Cambridge

An architectural guide

...

Helena Webster and Peter Howard
Photographs by John Niall MacLean

Cambridge

An architectural guide

• • • ellipsis

•••

BRITISH LIBRARY CATALOGUING IN PUBLICATION
A CIP record for this book is available from the British Library

PUBLISHED BY
Ellipsis London Limited
2 Rufus Street London N1 6PE
E MAIL ...@ellipsis.co.uk
WWW http://www.ellipsis.com
SERIES EDITOR Tom Neville
SERIES DESIGN Jonathan Moberly
IMAGE PROCESSING Bonie Venture
AUTHORS' PHOTOGRAPH Boyd
and Evans

COPYRIGHT © 2000 Ellipsis London
Limited

PRINTING AND·BINDING Hong Kong

ISBN 1 899858 47 4

Cambridge: an architectural guide

Helena Webster and Peter Howard 2000

Contents

Introduction

Cambridge is universally renowned for its University and colleges dating from the thirteenth century, and the sequence of gardens, now known as The Backs, that has been laid out over many years along the River Cam. The town owes its location, south of the flat East Anglian fenland that extends to the North Sea, to a historic crossing point on that river, the first from the sea.

The Romans established a station on rising land north of the river, around the present Castle Street area, to control the river crossing. Via Devana, preserved in the line that extends Huntingdon Road to Hills Road, crossed Akeman Street here, and in medieval times Roman bricks were reused in St Peter's church on Castle Street. Settlement of the spit of land south of the river started when Roman influence waned late in the fourth century. The name Grantebrycge, an early version of 'Cambridge', is first mentioned in 875. The tower of St Bene't's church dates from the end of the Anglo-Saxon period, before the Norman Conquest in 1066.

In c.1086 the Normans erected a motte-and-bailey castle on the higher land north of the river, where the Roman settlement had been. Although rebuilt with stone walls in 1286–91, the only reminder now is the castle mound. South of the river the main part of the town flourished around the High Street – today's Trinity Street, King's Parade and the first part of Trumpington Street – which was by then a narrow street built up along its full length on both sides. Trumpington Gate marked the town's southerly entrance, near Pembroke Street. A parallel street, Milne Street, ran along the line connecting Queens' Lane and Trinity Lane, but was later extinguished where it passed through King's and Trinity Colleges. Milne Street gave access to lanes leading to landing stages on the river, the town's western defence. To the east the town was protected by the man-made

King's Ditch, which traced a gentle arc from the river through present-day Mill Lane, Pembroke Street, Hobson Street and Park Street. This was improved in 1267 by Henry III. By then there were 14 churches in the close-knit town south of the river, of which 11 survive. The church of the Holy Sepulchre, or Round Church, though in part reconstructed, dates from the twelfth century; others were progressively remodelled in the medieval period.

In 1209, a migration of scholars from Oxford led to the establishment of the University. This corporation of learned men at first used existing churches and other buildings for convocations and teaching. Later, the Schools Building, started in the mid-fourteenth century, provided lecture rooms and libraries for the schools of Divinity, Civil Law and Canon Law, and a Senate House. It took the form of a two-storey court, a common form for larger buildings in the medieval period.

Soon, colleges were created by private, often royal, benefactors to house the teachers, while the students lived together in hostels and inns. By the end of the sixteenth century the hostels had all been incorporated into the colleges, where Fellows and students lived together, a situation that survives to the present. Some early colleges, including Peterhouse and Pembroke, were established outside the town gate, while Clare Hall (now Clare College), Trinity Hall, Gonville Hall (now Gonville and Caius College) and the original King's College formed a small group in the centre of town, close to the Schools Building and the University church of St Mary the Great. Although modified and refaced – and, in the case of Clare Hall, rebuilt – these colleges all survive in their original courtyard form on their original sites.

The late fifteenth-century suppression, and later dissolution in the early sixteenth century under Henry VIII, of Cambridge's religious houses

Cambridge: an architectural guide

provided sites for new colleges. Examples include Jesus College in the converted buildings of a Benedictine nunnery, St John's College on the site of the Hospital of St John the Evangelist, Magdalene College, which reused the buildings of a Benedictine college, and Sidney Sussex and Emmanuel Colleges. In the case of King's and Trinity Colleges, where the largest court of either Oxford or Cambridge was to be formed, space was found in the town through clearance of existing properties, closure of public thoroughfares and redevelopment of earlier halls and hostels.

Corpus Christi Old Court provides a comparatively unmodified example of a mid-fourteenth-century college, housed in a modest two-storey closed court, and using a nearby church, St Bene't, for its chapel. Queens' College, built in 1447–49 of brick – a favoured Cambridge building material – is a surviving textbook example of a later medieval college court. Queens' had its own chapel in the north range, a prominent turreted gate tower to mark the entrance, and the hall (which was used for communal meals), buttery and kitchen in the range opposite. A further freestanding range was later joined to the college to provide a pleasant three-sided cloister, a feature also retained from the earlier monastic buildings at Jesus College. The President's Lodge is by the dais end of the hall, adjoining the first-floor library and, as at St John's College and else-where, was later provided with a long gallery in imitation of grand houses. Other late-medieval gate towers are at Christ's, Trinity, St John's and Jesus Colleges; and the grandest of late medieval college chapels is, of course, at King's College. Here, the screen (1533–36) is a remarkably early and sophisticated example of Renaissance design, the new style recently imported under royal patronage from Italy.

From the mid-sixteenth to the mid-seventeenth centuries the three-sided court open on the fourth side became popular, following the example set in 1565–75 by Dr John Caius at Gonville and Caius College. Jesus, Emmanuel, Sidney Sussex, St Catharine's and Trinity College's cloistered Nevile's Court all followed this example, while at Christ's and Magdalene a court was implied by a freestanding building a short distance from the college. At Queens' and Emmanuel Colleges projecting single ranges were added to cope with increased student numbers. At this time too colleges were obtaining land on the west side of the river, leading to the growth of a series of gardens and meadows known as The Backs.

The architecture of this period, characterised by ornately gabled dormer windows, is best represented in David Loggan's *Cantabrigia Illustrata* (1690), a series of engraved aerial perspective views of the colleges. Caius Court, with its remarkable gates, Clare and St Catharine's Colleges, a small corner of Ivy Court at Pembroke College, and the 1640–43 Christ's Fellows' Building remain sufficiently unchanged to show the gradual supplanting of late Gothic details by typically Renaissance features such as pediments and pilasters, and cross-shaped mullion and transom windows displacing the late Tudor mullioned arched window. In 1623–24 St John's College library showed an early predilection for reviving the Gothic style, typifying the innate conservatism of much college architecture over the years. The chapel of 1628–32 at Peterhouse exhibited a curious mixture of Gothic, Jacobean and classical motifs, while introducing the idea of an open court.

It was the prominent young scientist Christopher Wren who in 1663–65 introduced to Cambridge the fully developed classical style of architecture with his first building, the chapel at Pembroke College. This was followed five years later with his more baroque chapel for Emmanuel College, where the cloistered screen was derived from that at Peterhouse. The library at Trinity College, a work of his maturity, also included a clois-

Cambridge: an architectural guide

tered walk, and also closed off a previously open court. Wren's proposals for a new Senate House and University Library alongside the Schools Building remained unrealised. Wren also promoted the wider use of ashlar-faced stonework.

Although a new street was created to link the University Church with the Schools Building as early as 1574, it was Nicholas Hawksmoor's unrealised visionary plans of 1712–13 for completing Henry VI's King's College and for replanning the town centre that might have transformed medieval Cambridge into a baroque city of forums, obelisks, vistas and grand buildings. James Gibbs also took up the challenge when in 1721 he proposed replacing the area of medieval housing between Great St Mary's and the Schools with new University buildings in the form of a three-sided classical court, and when, echoing Hawksmoor's plans, he made a similar proposal for King's College. In both cases lack of money and an innate reticence over grand schemes meant that only a single range resulted: the Senate House, and King's Fellows' Building. Stephen Wright's Palladian east range of the Schools Building (1754–58) provided the second side of the court by the Senate House, but indecision meant that despite later proposals by Matthew Brettingham, Robert Adam and John Soane, the third side was not completed. Instead, piecemeal house clearance along the west side of King's Parade and around Great St Mary's resulted, by the mid-nineteenth century, in the two classical University buildings around Senate House Yard, the late medieval University church and King's College chapel, and a small-scale town frontage meeting around an informal space in magnificent juxtaposition.

In the mid-eighteenth century James Burrough, the amateur architect and master of Gonville and Caius College, designed elegant classical buildings at Peterhouse and at Clare College. He and his acolyte successor

James Essex were both responsible for much classical refacing of medieval courts using ashlar stonework and sash windows, for example at Trinity Hall (Burrough, 1742–45) and at Christ's College (Essex, 1758–59). The classical style was redefined in the early nineteenth century by William Wilkins in his Greek Revival buildings for Downing College (1807–20), and by John Clement Mead's Greek Revival Observatory (1822–24). It reached its apotheosis in Charles Cockerell's personal and erudite University Library (1837–40), just the first range of a projected court to replace the Schools Building, and the Fitzwilliam Museum, built to designs by George Basevi in 1836–45, with later interiors by Edward Barry.

In 1821 Jeffry Wyatville revived the use of the late Tudor-Gothic style in his refacing of Sidney Sussex College. This style was enthusiastically embraced by William Wilkins in his reorganisation of Corpus Christi College of 1823–27, his inspired screen and court for King's, and his New Court for Trinity. These were followed in a similar style by Thomas Rickman and Henry Hutchinson's New Court at St John's College, with its delightful covered Gothic Revival bridge.

Whereas these schemes had really been classical buildings in late Gothic clothing, the Gothic Revival came of age in Cambridge with George Frederick Bodley's profound All Saints Church (1864) and George Gilbert Scott's striking chapel for St John's College, started the previous year. At the same time some colleges re-Gothicised their halls or chapels (for example Magdalene) by removing eighteenth-century plaster ceilings, and at Jesus College chapel Augustus Pugin returned the late Gothic chancel to its more 'authentic' early thirteenth-century form. William Morris was employed at Jesus, and at Peterhouse and Queens' College, to provide medieval-inspired decorative craftsmanship. Alfred Waterhouse, active in the colleges in the 1870s, used a rather dour Gothic

Revival at Girton, one of the new women's colleges, but opted for the early French Renaissance style both at Gonville and Caius' Tree Court and for the Red Building at Pembroke, where ironically he also replaced the original medieval hall with an ersatz Gothic Revival copy.

Basil Champneys also used Tudor-Gothic for the Selwyn Divinity School (1878–79), but for Newnham, the women's college he designed starting in 1875, he espoused the new and refreshing Queen Anne style made fashionable by Richard Norman Shaw and his followers. In a period of growing eclecticism Henry Hare married Tudor-Gothic and classical architecture in his building for Westminster College (1899), as did Thomas Jackson in 1904–11 in his Law School on the Downing Site, while by 1910 T H Lyon was drawing on Wren's work for his chapel interior for Sidney Sussex College.

In the town, red and dark brickwork had been used for the more prominent eighteenth-century houses, for example Little Trinity, Peterhouse Master's Lodge and Fitzwilliam House in Trumpington Street. As the town grew in the nineteenth century, residential developments preferred the local Cambridge stock 'white' brick: good examples are around Parker's Piece, at Maids' Causeway and New Square, in Fitzwilliam Street, and along the west end of Lensfield Road. Small suburbs of working-class housing grew up, for example, to the south at New Town. In the centre, the traditional pattern of street markets was replaced by a market square created by the clearance of old dwellings in front of the Guildhall, rebuilt in 1782 to designs by James Essex. The University, in the late nineteenth and early-twentieth centuries, created space for its expanding science departments by developing its old Botanic Garden north of Pembroke Street, now known as the New Museums Site, and a site to its south acquired in 1906 from Downing College.

In 1936–37 the Guildhall was again replaced, this time by one in a neo-Georgian style. Despite an unrealised scheme for Christ's College by Walter Gropius, the exiled head of the Bauhaus, a number of houses by George Checkley and the Mond Laboratory (1932–33) by H C Hughes, all owing something to the new International style, most interwar Cambridge architecture was wedded to the past. Magdalene College employed Edwin Lutyens; Christ's chose Albert Richardson in preference to Gropius; and Gonville and Caius College's St Michael's Court, designed by Murray Easton in 1934, is neo-Georgian where it faces the college, but more 'modern' on the Market Square side.

Clare College's Memorial Court (1923–34) and the new University Library (1931–34), both designed by Giles Gilbert Scott, share this conservatism. Their siting, to the west of The Backs, was a response to pressure on space in the central area. Other colleges followed this lead, and in the 1950s the University's arts faculties were sited there on the newly formed Sidgwick Site, as was Robinson College in 1977, Cambridge's most recent college. In 1999 the University adopted a master-plan for new science buildings on a substantial site further west. Post-war growth of the town, elevated to city status only in 1951, was in suburbs to its east and north, while the retail centre expanded first by the city centre redevelopment of Lion Yard (1975), and then to the east in the form of the Grafton Centre (1984). Cambridge now sits east of the newly constructed M11 from London, and south of the upgraded east–west A45 trunk road. These have defined new sites for Cambridge's burgeoning research-based employment (Michael Hopkins and Partners' Schlumberger Research Centre is an example), while relieving the city of through traffic. The centre has been partly pedestrianised and is served by park-and-ride schemes that cope well with Cambridge's growth both as a regional centre and a major tourist attraction. Barr Hill is a recent example of a planned settlement some 12 kilometres from the centre, and other such new 'villages' are currently either under construction or under consideration as Cambridge reviews its options for accommodating an ever-growing regional population.

In the latter half of the twentieth century both the colleges and the University have been prominent in commissioning the best new architecture, and Cambridge is now the best place in England for a good range of modern buildings in a small ambit, as this guide makes clear.

Queens' College started the recent phase of building new student accommodation in 1959 with the Erasmus Building by Basil Spence. Spence was followed by, among others, Powell and Moya at St John's and also at Queens'; Howell Killick Partridge and Amis at Darwin; Arup Associates for Corpus Christi and Trinity Hall; Denys Lasdun at Christ's; and Leslie Martin and Colin St John Wilson for Gonville and Caius, and Peterhouse. More recently MacCormac Jamieson Prichard and Wright have designed residences at Fitzwilliam and Trinity (twice), Allies and Morrison at Newnham, and Eric Parry at Pembroke. Five colleges – Newnham, Clare, Downing, St John's and Jesus – have built new libraries, while others have added other facilities, including Quinlan Terry's Howard Building at Downing and Michael Hopkins and Partners' Queen's Building at Emmanuel. Five colleges have been built from new since 1958, starting with Lasdun's Fitzwilliam College and Richard Sheppard, Robson and Partners' Churchill College. Together with Chamberlin Powell and Bon's New Hall, these explore the courtyard theme, while Ralph Erskine's Clare Hall and Gillespie Kidd and Coia's Robinson College provide variants on the theme.

The diversity of designs of recent buildings for the University is represented by James Stirling's History Faculty, Arup Associates' New Museums Building, John Outram's Judge Institute of Management Studies, and the Law Faculty by Sir Norman Foster and Partners. If all this makes Cambridge sound like an architectural zoo, it must be said that all these buildings do look well together and complement their historic setting. It must also be remembered that the colleges, the University and their benefactors, despite frequent periods of conservatism, have a long tradition – dating back to before King's College chapel – of commissioning outstanding architecture.

Using this book

The book's organisation has been made as straightforward as possible. Buildings are divided into five typological sections – the city (covering secular building), churches, the University, colleges, the last further split into two areas – with a sixth section covering the surrounding district. Buildings are ordered chronologically, except in the colleges sections where the order is alphabetical and then chronological under each college.

Below are some pointers to help you find your way around the colleges:

1. Cambridge University has three eight-week terms, running from early October to early December, mid-January to mid-March, and late April to mid-June. Some colleges have different opening times in term time and vacation time, and many are closed to visitors during the examination period in May and June.

2. Colleges are a law unto themselves. They can change their opening times, or decide to close to visitors at will.

3. In general colleges open their grounds, chapel and hall to visitors. There are private areas, which colleges expect to be treated as such. However, it may well be worth asking at the porter's lodge by the main gateway if you would like to see something not usually open to the public.

4. Many buildings are within walking distance of each other. However, you will probably need a street map for guidance. The best places to obtain one are the Tourist Information Centre, Wheeler Street, or one of the bookshops in King's Parade, Trinity Street and St John's Street.

Researching and writing this book has been an adventure and a great pleasure. We hope you enjoy Cambridge and its architecture as much as we do.

Helena Webster and Peter Howard

BIBLIOGRAPHY

Colvin, H M, *A Biographical Dictionary of British Architects, 1600–1840*, 3rd edn, Yale University Press, New Haven and London 1995

Loggan, D, *Cantabrigia Illustrata* [1690], ed. J W Clark, Macmillan & Bowes, Cambridge 1905

McKean, C, *Architectural Guide to Cambridge and East Anglia Since 1920*, RIBA Publications, London 1982

Pevsner, N, *The Buildings of England: Cambridgeshire*, 2nd edn, Penguin, Harmondsworth 1970

Rawle, T, *Cambridge Architecture*, Trefoil, London 1985

Ray, N, *Cambridge Architecture: A Concise Guide*, Cambridge University Press, Cambridge 1994

Roach, J P C (ed.), *Victoria History of the County of Cambridge and the Isle of Ely*, vol. 3: *City of Cambridge*, Oxford University Press, Oxford 1959

Royal Commission on Historical Monuments, *An Inventory of the Historical Monuments in the City of Cambridge*, parts I and II, HMSO, London 1939

Taylor, N, *Cambridge New Architecture*, 3rd edn, Leonard Hill, London 1970

Willis, R and Clark, J W, *The Architectural History of the University of Cambridge and the Colleges of Cambridge and Eton*, 3 vols, Cambridge University Press, Cambridge 1866 and 1988

The above works were used as primary source material in the preparation of this book, and we register our gratitude to their authors as well as to those who have been kind enough to help with further information. We apologise for inaccuracies that may, inadvertently, have crept into the text, and would be happy to be notified of them.

Cambridge: an architectural guide

The City

14 Trinity Street

Though much restored, this house is important because it is one of the few timber-framed domestic buildings surviving in Cambridge. Before 1893 the building was occupied by Foster's Bank and before that it was the Turk's Head Inn.

The elevation to Trinity Street has three storeys and an attic. It is composed of a modern ground-floor shop front above which are two symmetrical gabled bays, with the third storey and attic projecting. The upper section of each bay contains an oriel window with three transomed lights on the face and one in each canted side. The walls of the upper storeys are of exposed timber framing with pargeted infilling. This is modern but modelled on the original, displaying distinctive regional motifs. The turned timber columns, corbels supporting the jettying and the finials at the apex of the gables are particularly noteworthy.

The ground floor of the interior is modern. However, the upper floors still retain their cross and longitudinal chamfered ceiling beams.

ADDRESS 14 Trinity Street
ACCESS none; visible from the street

Early seventeenth century

Early seventeenth century

Eagle Inn

The Eagle Inn is typical of the many hostelries that filled the centre of Cambridge before the railway age. It has been in existence on the site probably since c.1530, and was formerly known as the Eagle and Child.

Numbers 6–9 Bene't Street have all at some time formed part of the inn. These buildings along the street frontage were refaced in a mixture of ashlar stone facing and render and given plain sash windows shortly before 1826, although they are of an earlier date. No. 8 contains a ground-floor room with early eighteenth-century panelling.

The carriageway to the side of No. 8 features on David Loggan's 1690 map of Cambridge, and leads to the coaching yard. The timber-framed range on the left of the yard was probably rebuilt c.1600. The open gallery giving access to the hostelry's rooms is probably an original feature, although the present gallery and windows date from c.1800. The end wing was rebuilt in the nineteenth century.

Conservation of the building in 1991–92 under the direction of Nick Cannell, when No. 8 was reincorporated into the inn, resulted in the uncovering of extensive wall painting and other historic features in the galleried range.

ADDRESS Bene't Street
ACCESS open Monday to Saturday, 11.00–23.00; Sunday, 11.00–22.30

Seventeenth–nineteenth centuries

Seventeenth–nineteenth centuries

Little Trinity

Nikolaus Pevsner poured praise on this building when he described it as 'perhaps the most handsome private house in Cambridge'. The stately Little Trinity was built in the early eighteenth century together with the humbler timber-framed kitchen block on the east side. The house is approached axially from Jesus Lane through iron gates of the same period, flanked by railings with brick and stone piers, and down a long grassed front court.

The front elevation of the house is symmetrical. It has five bays and is of three storeys plus a cellar. The central entrance is marked by a fine Georgian doorcase with a delicate fanlight, fluted Ionic pilasters and heavy pedimented entablature. The centre is further emphasised by the slight projection of the middle three bays of brickwork, which are surmounted by a simple broad pediment. The chimney stacks on the east and west gables complete the symmetrical composition. The main material is dark brick in header bond with rubbed red brick dressings around the double-hung sash windows and on the corners. Ashlar is used for the string courses, cornice, pediment, copings and rooftop urns.

The interior plan has just two rooms on each floor with a central hall leading to a staircase bay applied to the rear elevation. The broad oak staircase and some of the original panelling and fireplaces remain.

ADDRESS 16 Jesus Lane
ACCESS none; visible from Jesus Lane and Park Street

c.1725

c.1725

Railway Station

The central arcaded portion is all that remains of the complex designed by Francis Thompson for Eastern Counties Railway Company. The station was originally built with a second identical arcaded building east of the present one. It was intended that vehicles would draw up within the west range and trains within the east range. A second timber platform was added to the east in 1850. In 1863 two-storey ranges were added to the north and south of the west arcade, and the east arcade and timber platform were removed to make way for the present unusual arrangement of a single platform serving trains going in both directions. In the interim there have been minor alterations, such as the lengthening of the platform, but the exterior of the west entrance arcade remains virtually unchanged.

Thompson was a well-known railway architect who designed stations, large and small, for Eastern Counties on the Chester to Holyhead line as well as on the London to Cambridge line. He often worked in the Italianate style and his best-known work is the red-brick Chester Station of 1848. Thompson's Italianate design for Cambridge consists of a long 15-bay single-storey arcade built in Cambridgeshire stock brick with stone dressings. The distinctive heavy crowning entablature has an architrave enriched with small plain roundels, a frieze with raised metopes alternating with shaped brackets and a wide overhanging cornice. The spandrels contain roundels displaying the arms of the town, various dignitaries and some of the colleges.

ADDRESS Station Road, off Hills Road
ACCESS public areas open most hours

Francis Thompson 1845–47

Francis Thompson 1845–47

Corn Exchange

In the late Victorian period Gothic was a popular style for commercial buildings, and for Richard Reynolds Rowe, then surveyor to the City of Cambridge, an eclectic mixture of Venetian Gothic and Italianate seemed appropriate for the new Corn Exchange.

Rowe's design is not as inventive or fluent as Waterhouse's Foster's Bank in Sidney Street (1891) but it nevertheless demonstrates an understanding of John Ruskin's demands for rationalist planning, structural expression and embodied decoration. Viewed from the corner of Corn Exchange Street and Wheeler Street the building's form clearly expresses its internal arrangement: a nave-like hall with an attached entrance block and corner staircase. A symmetrical façade of three bays faces Wheeler Street. The central entrance bay projects slightly for emphasis, and the gable at roof level is curiously surmounted by a chimney stack. To each side, two-storey arched recesses contain windows linked by terracotta panels depicting agricultural scenes. The elevation to Corn Exchange Street is articulated like a church nave with large arch-headed windows at ground-floor level, more terracotta panels and a sequence of small arch-headed clerestory windows above. The blue and red polychromy of the brick arch-heads to the windows and connecting string courses, set against Cambridge stock brick, contributes to the Venetian Gothic flavour.

The large hall inside has an impressive iron and glass roof. However, recent internal alterations made to facilitate the building's use as a concert venue have largely spoilt its original spatial quality.

ADDRESS Wheeler Street, Corn Exchange Street
ACCESS open Monday to Saturday 10.00–16.00 and evenings for performances

Richard Reynolds Rowe 1874

Corn Exchange

Richard Reynolds Rowe 1874

Westminster College

In 1893 Henry T Hare won the competition for a new town hall in Oxford with a showy neo-Jacobean proposal that owed something to the work of the architect Thomas Jackson, his mentor. By 1895, when the acceptance of a site in Cambridge prompted the Presbyterian Westminster College to move out of London, Hare designed for them an altogether more restrained and accomplished building.

Four generous Tudor-style oriel windows across the main façade set the tone for the building. These alternate with small windows to give the elevation a measured rhythm, which is amplified by the use of stone dressings set against walls of dark red brick. However, the seventeenth-century detailing of the small windows, decorative cartouches and doorcase to the entrance, and the small triangular dormers in dark oak that peer between widely spaced slots in the solid parapet show that this is no ordinary neo-Tudor design.

A massive tower rises to one side. This has an obelisk on a corner buttress, and is given monumentality by the way it diminishes in size and is made of stone towards the top. Like the Oxford town hall, an inventive cupola in dark oak crowns it. The tower contains a grand staircase that leads up from near the segmentally roofed dining hall behind. A transverse corridor serves the rooms in the main block and gives access to a small ground-floor chapel at the rear of the building. This was added in 1921, and its low vaulted roof and warm oak panelling give it a comfortably intimate quality.

ADDRESS Madingley Road, by Northampton Street
ACCESS limited access: enquire at office; visible from Madingley Road

Henry T Hare 1895–99

Henry T Hare 1895–99

48 Storey's Way

Mackay Hugh Baillie Scott spent much of his life promoting the Arts and Crafts ethic. In 1906 he published *House and Gardens* in which he suggested that an open living space, derived from the medieval hall house, was the key to a well-planned house, and that beauty was derived both from fitness for purpose and the honest use of craft techniques. 48 Storey's Way, commissioned by Herbert Ainslie Roberts, head of the University Appointments Board, is one of Baillie Scott's finest houses and is a superb illustration of his theories.

The basic form of the building, a two-storey rectangular plan under a long steeply pitched roof, is remarkably straightforward. Rather unusually for a picturesque composition the plan is arranged about a central axis which runs from the front gate, through the house, to the far end of the garden. However, on the street elevation symmetry is defied by the addition of two unequal gables. The garden elevation is more formal and is dominated by a roof with an unbroken eaves line and two ground-floor bay windows placed symmetrically about the central axis. The materials, brick, render, oak and tile, give the house an Arts and Crafts quality. The garden design, also by Baillie Scott, is reminiscent of a Kate Greenaway book illustration.

Internally, the main south-facing living area consists of four linked spaces: a dining room, an inglenook fireplace, a study and a kitchen. Four bedrooms on the first floor mirror the major spaces below. The interior use of exposed oak beams and panelling, white painted decorative plasterwork, and leaded lights continues the Arts and Crafts tradition.

ADDRESS 48 Storey's Way (Nos 29, 30, 54, 56 are also by Baillie Scott)
ACCESS none; visible from the street

Mackay Hugh Baillie Scott 1912–13

Mackay Hugh Baillie Scott 1912–13

White House

In the 1930s the Modern style found an outlet primarily in rare commissions for private houses by progressive or eccentric individuals. Conduit Head Road contains four houses in a row from the period: White House, by George Checkley, the adjacent Salix, formerly known as Brandon House (1934), by H C Hughes, Thurso House (1932) again by Checkley, and finally, the weather-boarded Shawms (1938) by Justin Blanco White. White House was the first and was built for Checkley's own occupation.

The house looks like the Osbert Lancaster cartoon of the 'twentieth-century functional' house. It is a two-storey symmetrical block with a roof-top pavilion. The front door is placed centrally and flanked by strip windows divided into sections by the concrete structural frame. All the ingredients of a modern house are present: sharp lines, white painted render, *fenêtres en longueur* (strip windows), roof terrace and nautical railings, yet somehow the design remains rather naïve in comparison with its European precedents.

Internally, the spatial planning is unremarkable. Checkley's second house in Conduit Head Road, Thurso House, is more dynamic with a double-height living room and a curved stair dividing the living area from the dining area. Sadly, White House is in a state of disrepair. Its status as one of the earliest modern houses in Cambridge, and indeed in England, makes it deserving of careful restoration.

ADDRESS 1 Conduit Head Road, off Madingley Road
ACCESS none; visible from entrance drive off Conduit Head Road

George Checkley 1930–31

George Checkley 1930–31

Highsett

Nikolaus Pevsner pronounced this small development of high-class private housing 'the best housing group in Cambridge'. It was built in the 1950s by Span, a system-build development company. Pevsner, an apologist for the New Empiricism, saw it as representing a new model for urban dwelling, one based on two separate English traditions: the terraced house and the picturesque garden.

The first phase of the development, facing Hills Road, is a formal three-storey court of flats. To the rear of these are the second and third phases consisting of an informal arrangement of two- and three-storey terraces. The initial design also included a 15-storey tower set in the garden between the court and the terraces, but this was subsequently abandoned. The site plan plays down the importance of street and car, structuring the circulation around sinuous pedestrian paths and extensive planting. The effect is picturesque, exactly as intended. The court is architecturally the most accomplished. Here the building typology is radical, and there are moments of architectural delight such as the glimpsed view of the land-scaped court from Hills Road and the delicate glazed screens that enclose the communal entrances to the flats. The architecture of the subsequent phases is rather lame by comparison and continues Lyons' standard vocabulary of brick cross-wall construction, concrete floor slabs, flat roofs and cladding of brick, timber boarding and arrowhead tiles.

ADDRESS 45 Hills Road, opposite Bateman Street
ACCESS external public spaces only

Eric Lyons and Partners 1958–60, 1962, 1963–64

Eric Lyons and Partners 1958–60, 1962, 1963–64

2–2a Granchester Road

At the time these houses were built the architect was a lecturer at the School of Architecture and had a young practice in Cambridge. This modest building, a terrace of two houses, one for the architect and the other for the university lecturer Peter Squire, can be seen as furthering the preoccupations of Colin St John Wilson's earlier projects with Leslie Martin, including Harvey Court (see page 5.34), as well as his extension to the School of Architecture (see page 3.20).

The unified loggia-like façade, reminiscent of Harvey Court, screens the entrances to the two houses. Each house contains a similar grouping of rooms; they are essentially three-bedroomed houses. However, the Wilson house has a double-height living space and a studio at the front. The plans are L-shaped, with the living rooms projecting into the garden to create walled patios. An inventive section in the Wilson house connects the upper floor with the double-height living room via a Le Corbusier-inspired metal staircase and library gallery. Roof-lights set into the flat roof bring light into the centre of the deep plan.

A description of the plan does little to communicate the power of this little building. Wilson employed a modular system to determine the size and location of every element. The rigour of its application is communicated through the display of the materials of the building's construction. Thus, it is the module of the fair-faced concrete block, used inside and out, that provides the dominant aesthetic. The whole atmosphere is tough and elemental, reflecting the architect's Brutalist allegiances.

ADDRESS 2–2a Granchester Road
ACCESS none; visible from the street

Colin St John Wilson 1961–64

Colin St John Wilson 1961–64

Radcliffe Court

This mixed development of shops and 15 flats represents a period of architecture when the International Style was promoted as appropriate for any context, even a picturesque market square. The development, which is much larger than its frontage suggests, filled a long under-developed plot within the urban block.

However, it is the façade to the Market Square that is really interesting. In some senses the composition is a sensitive response to context: the building follows the street line, and its storey heights and overall height reflect those of its neighbours. Also, its uses accord with the surrounding mixed-use typology (commercial on the ground and first floors; residential on the upper floors). Yet the architecture of white-painted in-situ concrete with bays articulated in a sawtooth manner to face south and the view of St Mary's Church is uncompromisingly modernist. Its architectural tone is light and both the whiteness and the balconies are vaguely reminiscent of the seaside and of Mediterranean building. Nikolaus Pevsner records that the elevation was restyled by the City Architect's Department before planning permission was given, which places it firmly in the period before the idea of 'blending-in' was dominant within planning authorities.

ADDRESS Market Hill, and 7 Rose Crescent
ACCESS none; visible from the street

Stanley R Neville and Partners 1964

Stanley R Neville and Partners 1964

Schlumberger Research Centre

Schlumberger Cambridge Research Ltd provides technical services to companies involved in oil exploration. Michael Hopkins' brief was for a building to house research facilities and his design stressed the integration of functions.

Distant views of the building are puzzling but eye-catching. The symmetrical sectional profile, as seen from Madingley Road, seems to allude to some great animal or insect. This first phase is a direct expression of its different functions. It consists of a 24-metre-wide by 10-metre-high central space used for drill rig testing, which also contains the main reception, restaurant and library, flanked by two single-storey wings containing laboratory spaces and offices. The central area is covered by a vast tripartite Teflon-coated fibreglass tent supported from paired masts by tensioned cables. The single-storey wings have external portals, consisting of tubular steel columns and external lattice beams, which support profiled steel flat roofs and walls made of sliding glass doors.

Phase two to the south consists of two pavilions with central atria, linked by a glass entrance on axis with phase one. The first-floor structure consists of prefabricated ferroconcrete floor slabs, inspired by the work of the Italian architect Pier Luigi Nervi, supported on tubular steel columns. A 3.6-metre glazing module with distinctive black horizontal blinds forms the enclosure. The central atria have innovative pneumatically supported roofs made from three layers of transparent fluorocarbon film.

ADDRESS High Cross Research Park, Madingley Road
ACCESS none; visible from the street

Michael Hopkins and Partners 1982–85, 1990–92

Michael Hopkins and Partners 1982–85, 1990–92

Quayside

In 1983 Magdalene College invited designs for Quayside, the site facing the college across the river, on the town bank. The site had operated as a commercial quay until the beginning of the twentieth century and was occupied by a jumble of workshops and sheds, two modest commercial buildings adjacent to Bridge Street and a range of fine early nineteenth-century houses facing Thompson's Lane. The college's brief asked for a mixed development of shops, restaurants, offices and student residences.

Quayside is a skilful essay in picturesque urban design and low-key contextual architecture. The accommodation is divided into a number of ranges, with shops and restaurants on the ground floor and offices above, arranged around an informal public space that opens off a new pedestrian river walk. Each range is given an individual architectural character and uses different materials in an attempt to replicate the accretive nature of the surrounding town fabric. In fact, just one architect designed the development, and the variety of façades conceals a uniform steel structural frame. Through the central archway, marked by the college arms, is a second smaller courtyard bounded on three sides with shops and offices. Its fourth, east, side is formed by the rear of the nineteenth-century houses on Thompson's Lane, refurbished to provide student accommodation. A pedestrian route continues from the court through to Thompson's Lane.

Beyond the development, through the loggia with double gables alluding to the Pepys Building (see page 4.54), the river walk continues past the high-density urban housing by Dixon Del Pozzo (1986) to Jesus Green.

ADDRESS Bridge Street
ACCESS public spaces open all hours

Hughes and Bicknell, succeeded by Nicholas Ray Associates 1983–89

Hughes and Bicknell, succeeded by Nicholas Ray Associates 1983–89

Cambridge Regional College

Cambridge Regional College, Cambridge's largest college of further education, was built as a phased campus development on a difficult 9.5-hectare site on the northern fringes of the city's suburbs. Three phases are complete: a two-storey hall and recreational block adjacent to the entrance, with a library and business studies courtyard block (1993), a similar central administration, science and technology block and, most recently, a three-storey general education range. Bernard Stilwell was the director of the Powell Moya Partnership responsible for the master-plan and design of the first two phases, while the latest phase was designed by his own practice.

The creation of an axial route or street linking the first three phases, and the ability to create inviting public places both inside and around the buildings, relate this project to the concerns that characterised the earlier work of Powell and Moya, for example at St John's College Cripps Building (see page 4.74). So does the evident love of exposing the tectonics of the construction.

However, there are also noticeable differences. The client's insistence on the use of brick walls and pitched roofs, and the need to work to a more finely tuned budget have resulted in buildings that are no less distinctive. A far greater range of materials and colours is used than in Powell and Moya's earlier buildings: yellow brickwork, steel windows, slate roofs and concrete columns are contrasted with natural timber roof beams, glass curtain walling, and brightly coloured rendered and tiled panels. This gives the scheme a light-hearted and possibly more youthful and 'European' flavour, which is well suited to its use.

ADDRESS King's Hedges Road
ACCESS college open Monday to Friday, 8.30–16.30; apply at reception

Powell Moya Partnership 1993–95, Bernard Stilwell Architects 1997

Powell Moya Partnership 1993–95, Bernard Stilwell Architects 1997

Churches

St Bene't

The tower of St Bene't (its name a shortened version of St Benedict) is the oldest building in Cambridge, dating, as do the four corners of the originally aisleless nave and the south wall of the chancel, from the second quarter of the eleventh century. The tower's three receding stages, 'long-and-short' quoins (consisting of narrow stones placed with the long sides alternately upright and horizontal) and small arched openings with heavy recessed baluster columns on the uppermost stage are all characteristic of Carolingian influence on Anglo-Saxon work preceding the Norman Conquest. Inside, the tower arch to the nave is perfectly preserved. Here long-and-short work is curiously married with slender attached columns, while above the entablature the arch mouldings spring from the backs of lion-like beasts. A contemporary arched doorway survives above.

In the thirteenth century, lancet windows were added to the south wall of the chancel, and following a fire the chancel arch and nave arcades were rebuilt in their present form at the turn of the fourteenth century. The present timber nave roof – and probably the clerestory – date from 1452. Following the foundation of Corpus Christi College (see page 5.4) in 1352 on a site south of the church, St Bene't was used as the college chapel until, in 1579, the college built its own. The south vestry, a small chapel above, and the gallery and gateway linking them to the college all date from 1487 to 1515.

In 1853, the north aisle with its attractive timber roof was rebuilt and widened, and a porch added, to designs by J R Brandon, while Arthur Blomfield rebuilt and widened the south aisle in 1872.

ADDRESS Bene't Street
ACCESS daily, 7.45–18.15

Early eleventh and thirteenth–nineteenth centuries

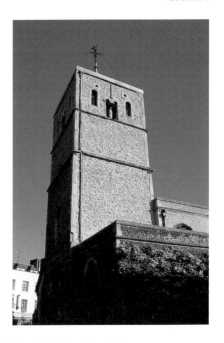

Early eleventh and thirteenth–nineteenth centuries

Holy Sepulchre (The Round Church)

In 1099 Jerusalem fell to the first Crusade and the rotunda erected by Constantine in the fourth century over the supposed tomb of Christ, the Anastasis, was reconstructed. In imitation of this rotunda, round churches were built in England by the Orders founded to guard the Holy Land and the Holy Sepulchre. Five survive, including that at Cambridge.

Sometime between 1113 and 1140 the graveyard of an earlier church was granted to 'the fraternity of the Holy Sepulchre', a local guild, to build a 'monasterium' in honour of God and the Holy Sepulchre. A circular church with eight massive columns, a surrounding ambulatory and possibly an apse to the east was constructed in the style now known as Romanesque. In the fifteenth century the church was enlarged to the east with a rectangular chancel, with a chapel on its north side. At the same time the drum of the round church was extended upwards to form a tall battlemented belfry, and its windows were enlarged.

In 1841 part of the ambulatory collapsed, and a drastic restoration was initiated by the High Church Cambridge Camden Society, under the direction of the architect Anthony Salvin. From 1841 to 1843 Salvin replaced the belfry with the present conical roof, under which he constructed a stone vault, and replaced the clerestory windows. He rebuilt the ambulatory vault, replacing the windows with others in the Romanesque style and rebuilt the west doorway. Salvin added a bell turret, and built a south aisle to match the north chapel, which he also reconstructed.

ADDRESS Sidney Street, on the corner of Round Church Street
ACCESS generally daily, 12.00–17.00

Early twelfth century and later

Early twelfth century and later

St Mary Magdalene

St Mary Magdalene was built in the mid-twelfth century as the chapel of the St Mary Magdalene leper hospital at Stourbridge, about 2.5 kilometres east of the city centre. The hospital ceased to function by 1279, but had already become the site of Stourbridge Fair, for over five centuries one of the country's largest trade fairs. The chapel survived largely unaltered as ancillary accommodation for the fair until the university acquired it in 1817, after which it was restored.

St Mary Magdalene is a rare survival of a small Norman chapel whose construction and decoration, though modest, are typical of the pre-Gothic period. The chapel consists of a small rectangular nave with a smaller rectangular chancel. This is separated from the nave by a semi-circular chancel arch with chevron decoration. The nave is of flint rubble, which would originally have been plastered externally, accentuating the stone string courses and corner shafts. The north and south arched doorways and narrow windows are original, but the central window on the west gable is nineteenth century. The chancel is of stone construction and was originally vaulted in stone. Its east window and south doorway are nineteenth century. Both chancel and nave were given their timber roofs c.1400.

ADDRESS Newmarket Road, before Ditton Walk
ACCESS key available – see noticeboard

Mid-twelfth century

Mid-twelfth century

St Edward King and Martyr

This charming and compact church stands between King's Parade and Peas Hill. The lower part of the west tower and the tower arch inside the church are the only visible remains of an earlier thirteenth-century aisle-less church. A new nave, chancel arch and aisles were built in the early fifteenth century. The church grew further in 1466 with the addition of the chancel arcades and the north and south chapels, when the church was appropriated by Henry VI for use as a chapel by Trinity Hall and Clare College following their loss of the use of St John Zachary. It is probable that the windows on the south side of the church date from the late seventeenth or early eighteenth century, and the vestry was added in 1846. George Gilbert Scott restored the church in 1858–60, and redesigned the east and west windows and the west door. Minor restoration occurred again in 1869, 1939 and 1946, the last being directed by Albert Richardson. The heraldic stained glass dates from the 1946 restoration.

What is seen today retains its early fifteenth-century character. Externally, the form clearly displays its constituent parts – nave, chancel, aisles, chapels, vestry and tower. The walls are of rubble with Barnack stone dressings, with some rendering of the tower. The nave is flanked by an arcade of four bays of delicate piers with thin, semi-octagonal shafts and concave sides, and two-centred arches. The north and south chapels are unusual on plan for encroaching on one bay of the aisles. The chancel roof is fifteenth century. Of the fittings, the wall tablets and ledger slabs are good and the Latimer Pulpit (c.1510) has fine linenfold panelling.

ADDRESS St Edward's Passage
ACCESS daily, 12.00–15.00

Early thirteenth and early fifteenth centuries

Early thirteenth and early fifteenth centuries

St Mary the Less

The church had a pre-Conquest foundation and, in response to its location in the medieval town, was originally called St Peter without Trumpington Gates. The ashlar building seen today dates from the 1340–52 rebuilding when it was reconsecrated as St Mary the Less. Peterhouse, the adjacent college (see page 5.64) took its name from the original church, which it used until 1632 when a chapel was built in First Court. The church was entered directly from the college by a gallery south of the chancel, adjacent to the fifteenth-century vestry.

The fourteenth-century building was a single volume of five bays combining nave and chancel, leaving the original tower at the north-west corner. At some date the tower fell, and the base was rebuilt in the nineteenth century incorporating fragments of the original work to provide the main entrance to the church. There may have been plans to add a transverse antechapel in the position of the larger sixth bay, making the plan like that of the Oxford college chapels, but in the fifteenth century the sixth bay was built in its present form. In the north and south walls are the remains of two fifteenth-century chantry chapels, of which only the openings survive. The nave and chancel have large two-centred, four-light arched windows with a six-light east window, all of which have good Decorated Gothic tracery. Of the fittings, there is a Perpendicular Gothic font; the pulpit is of 1741. Ninian Comper designed the altar setting in the twentieth century.

George Gilbert Scott restored the church in 1856–91 and the chapel in the south wall of the nave was designed by T H Lyon in 1931.

ADDRESS Trumpington Street, Little St Mary's Lane
ACCESS daily, during daylight hours

Mid-fourteenth and fifteenth centuries

Mid-fourteenth and fifteenth centuries

Holy Trinity

Holy Trinity is famous for its connection with the Evangelical Movement that began with Charles Simeon's ministry from 1782 to 1836. The church contains an 1836 monument to Simeon by Humphrey Hopper. The chronology of the building is somewhat complex resulting in an architectural composition that lacks cohesion. Nevertheless, the church is interesting for the display of architectural elements from almost every century since 1350.

The first church on the site was of timber and was burnt down in the huge town fire of 1174. The second simple stone church with nave and chancel was begun soon after and was significantly enlarged in 1350 with the widening of the nave, the building of the west tower within the west end of the nave, and the addition of north and south aisles. The north and south arcades of the nave with their small internal arches springing from the moulded capitals of quatrefoil piers date from this time. The north porch, nave, clerestory and transepts were added in the late fifteenth century, and the nave and transept ceilings have fine four-centred transverse arches. The transepts have particularly large two-centred, six-light end windows and two tiers of side windows. Early in the sixteenth century the south aisle was widened and its windows date from that time. The gallery in the south transept was added in 1836 and the stained glass by W H Constable in 1855. The chancel was rebuilt in 1834 and the decoration, by George Frederick Bodley, was carried out in 1885. The spire was rebuilt in 1901.

ADDRESS Market Street
ACCESS during term Monday to Friday, 9.00–17.00; closed in August

Mid-fourteenth–twentieth centuries

Mid-fourteenth–twentieth centuries

St Mary the Great

Great St Mary's, the University Church, is first mentioned in 1205, but it was rebuilt with university funding while King's College Chapel (see page 5.36) was under construction. Like other great East Anglian Perpendicular Gothic churches, it has a tall, slender nave arcade, of five bays, surmounted by a generous clerestory. The two-centred arches and finely carved spandrel panels are enclosed by rectangular frames, all carved out of clunch, a hard chalk, and originally painted. The slim shafts are extended upwards to support a shallow timber roof, completed in 1506. A timber rood screen, now removed, originally separated the nave from the chancel. Externally, the church is dominated by a massive square tower, and is characterised by the tall, almost rectangular, aisle windows and battlemented parapets.

The tower, from which there is a fine view, was designed to stand proud of the church, but the aisles were extended each side of it in the early sixteenth century. When, nearly a century later, the upper two stages were built, still using the Perpendicular Gothic style, the plan for a tall spire remained unrealised. The original Elizabethan classical west doorway was replaced in 1850 by one in the High Victorian Gothic Revival style.

The aisle galleries were added in 1735 to a design by the Italianate architect James Gibbs. In 1766 James Essex altered the windows in the north chapel and aisle, while in 1783 he sensitively secured the original nave roof that his father had repaired in 1726 by supporting it from a new roof above. The present south porch was built in 1888; the tracery of the east window is also nineteenth century.

ADDRESS St Mary's Passage
ACCESS Monday to Saturday, 10.00–16.30; Sunday, 12.30–16.30

rebuilt 1478–1519, tower completed 1593–1608

rebuilt 1478–1519, tower completed 1593–1608

All Saints

All Saints was built as a replacement for the medieval church of All Saints that formerly stood in St John's Street opposite Trinity College chapel. This church was demolished in 1865 when the street was widened.

George Frederick Bodley favoured English Gothic, as opposed to the French influence of some of his contemporaries, and the church, his second design for the site, is an essay in the late thirteenth- and early fourteenth-century Decorated style. A lofty nave, supported by gabled buttresses, has to its south an almost equally tall, single aisle. The nave is separated from the choir by a rood beam added in 1871 as a structural part of the massive tower above. The rood screen below dates from 1904. As befitted a church designed on High Church Tractarian principles, the nave, lacking a clerestory, is dark and mysterious, while beyond the choir and tower the projecting sanctuary and raised high altar are bathed in light from the large east window. The tower and prominent spire, completed in 1869–71, are based on those of the church at Ashbourne, Derbyshire, constructed in 1320–40.

Bodley called on William Morris, with whom he was then working at Jesus College chapel (see page 4.44), to design the rich internal decorative scheme. Morris provided the stencilled wall and roof decorations, and together with the Pre-Raphaelites Edward Burne-Jones and Ford Madox Brown he designed the figures in the east window. The floor in the choir has encaustic tiles made by Minton. Various items, including the fifteenth-century font, were brought from the original church.

ADDRESS Jesus Lane, by Manor Street
ACCESS key available – see noticeboard

George Frederick Bodley 1864

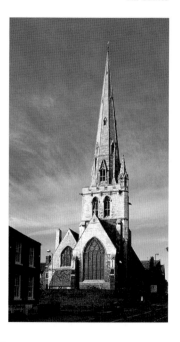

George Frederick Bodley 1864

Our Lady and the English Martyrs

This vast Roman Catholic church was paid for by Yolande Duvernay, the operatic dancer, and was dedicated to Our Lady of the Assumption and the English Martyrs who died for the faith between 1535 and 1681. It was designed by the Newcastle architects Archibald Matthias Dunn and Edward Joseph Hansom, who were known for their Catholic church architecture. Although much less well known than George Frederick Bodley's All Saints (see page 2.16) or George Gilbert Scott's chapel at St John's College (see page 4.72), its architecture is a fine example of High Victorian Gothic Revival. The church is a cruciform structure of impressive, cathedral-like proportions. The buttressed polygonal apse, square tower over the crossing and tower over the north-west porch with its tall spire form an imposing pile, and the spire is a prominent landmark.

Internally, the church has an almost standard English Gothic cruciform plan with tall clerestoried nave, lower north and south aisles, a crossing and crossing tower, wide transepts and a more French than English polygonal apse. Another unusual feature is the transverse antechapel at the west end that repeats the Oxford model used by Scott at St John's. The detailing is consistently early Decorated, from the reticulated tracery of the windows to the elaborate stone tierceron-vaulted nave roof. Particularly quirky is the octagonal pier separating the transepts from the crossing. Most of the carving and statuary is contemporary with the building and is by Boulton of Cheltenham. The stained glass in the west window depicts the English Martyrs and is by Powell & Co.

ADDRESS Hills Road, Lensfield Road
ACCESS daily, 7.30–18.30

Archibald Matthias Dunn and Edward Joseph Hansom 1885–90

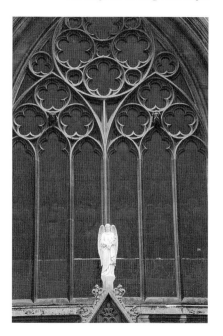

Archibald Matthias Dunn and Edward Joseph Hansom 1885–90

The University

The Old Schools

The Old Schools were built by the University to house lecture rooms on the ground floor with libraries above. Over the centuries the University Library and museums took over and expanded the whole complex until the Library moved to new premises (see page 3.16) in 1934. The buildings are now used for general University purposes and administration.

The Old Schools now consist of two courts. The east court is the site of the original Schools, while the west court, now the main entrance, is a nineteenth-century redevelopment of King's College Old Court, acquired by the University in 1829. With the exception of the east range (see page 3.6), which was rebuilt in 1754–58, the east court is late medieval, and is constructed of rubble stonework with four centred windows and tiered buttresses. The north range, completed in 1400, was built to house the Divinity School, with the Senate House and a chapel above. The west range, completed in 1454, housed the Canon Law School, while the south range of 1457–c.1470 housed the Civil Law School. Its third storey was added in 1864–67. The east range formed the original entrance opposite the area of housing which, until it was cleared in the eighteenth century, occupied the space between the east range and the University Church.

The redevelopment of the west court started with the construction of a new University Library in 1837–40 on the north side. George Gilbert Scott rebuilt the south range in 1862, while in 1887–90 John Pearson closed the court on the Trinity Lane side, incorporating and completing the 1441 unfinished gatehouse of King's College. This and the south range are both in a Victorian late-medieval style.

ADDRESS Trinity Lane
ACCESS none; visible from the tower of St Mary the Great

Fourteenth, fifteenth, eighteenth and nineteenth centuries

Fourteenth, fifteenth, eighteenth and nineteenth centuries

The Senate House

The proposal to build a new Senate House on part of the land between The Old Schools and the University Church, then occupied by housing, resulted from the increased growth of the University Library in the Schools Building (see page 3.2). The University asked James Gibbs to comment on a first design by James Burrough. Gibbs, who had been a pupil to Carlo Fontana in Rome, responded by designing a grand classical three-sided court facing St Mary the Great, the three sides consisting of the Senate House, a matching Registry and Printing House opposite, and a new library joining them. Only the Senate House was built to Gibbs's designs, and its unfinished west end was completed by James Essex in 1767–68. The area of housing was gradually cleared, and finally turfed and paved in 1792, when Gibbs' massive cast-iron railings were extended along its east side to form Senate House Yard.

Gibbs' building is a single rectangular volume of Portland stone raised on a podium. Giant Corinthian pilasters, paired at the corners, separate the windows, while pediments supported by attached columns mark the entrances on the east end and the south side. The windows are on two storeys, the lower with alternating triangular and segmental pediments, the upper arched and corresponding to an internal gallery. The gallery and lower part of the hall, including the western dais and the eastern entry under the gallery, are panelled in dark timber. This complements the white coffered plasterwork of the ceiling by the Italians Artari and Bagutti and the original black-and-white marble paving.

ADDRESS King's Parade
ACCESS none; visible from the street

James Gibbs 1722–30

James Gibbs 1722–30

The Old Schools, East Range

Twenty-two years after the completion of the Senate House (see page 3.4) the University considered building the west range of James Gibbs's projected court to house the Royal Library bequeathed by George I. Concerned about the impact on nearby Caius Court (see page 4.32), James Burrough instead prepared a scheme for redeveloping the fifteenth-century east range of the Schools Building (see page 3.2), to the rear of Gibbs's proposed library range.

After the intervention of the Chancellor, the First Duke of Newcastle, his protégé Stephen Wright was appointed architect. Wright had worked for William Kent and was one of the architects promoted by Lord Burlington and his circle who had revived the style of the sixteenth-century Italian architect Andrea Palladio. Wright made a proposal for completing the court, though only the library was built, in the position proposed by Burrough.

Wright's building, while retaining Gibbs's use of Portland stone, is far prettier and lacks the gravity of the Senate House. The library block of five bays projects forward over a loggia with rusticated arches, which originally went through the building at each side. The upper-floor windows are contained within arches, the central window having three lights in the Venetian manner. Above is a frieze of swags, a theme repeated in the internal plasterwork, and urns on a balustraded cornice. The rear elevation is similar but lacks the loggia and the decorative elements. To each side a screen with a similar Venetian window masks the ends of the north and south ranges of the late-medieval Schools Building, that to the south range concealing Wright's new staircase.

ADDRESS King's Parade
ACCESS none; visible from the street

Stephen Wright 1754–58

Stephen Wright 1754–58

The University

Observatory

The first Cambridge Observatory was over the Great Gate at Trinity College (see page 4.82) and was demolished in 1797. In 1821 a University syndicate launched a competition for the design of a new observatory to be modelled on the one at the Cape of Good Hope. John Clement Mead won the competition with a Greek Revival design, a style not unreasonably deemed appropriate for a structure intended for scientific purposes.

Mead's symmetrical design consists of a south-facing central block containing the observatory and main entrance, which is connected to two Observers' houses by ranges housing workrooms. The central block is designed as a monumental tetrastyle pedimented Doric portico sitting on a stylobate of three steps leading to the entrance doorway, which has a characteristic Greek Revival tapered architrave. Above is a most un-Greek central copper dome on a square attic. The elevations of the adjoining ranges appear disappointingly flat, despite attempts to introduce modelling by dividing them into bays, adding rustication, and giving the principal windows architraves and entablatures. The main elevations of the Observers' houses are also symmetrical but are made to appear less monumental by omitting the main Doric frieze, using rustication only up to the first floor, increasing the size of the windows and omitting architraves, except around the entrances.

Internally, the interesting central block has a wide circular passageway with deep alcoves on the diagonal giving access to the stairs and workrooms. This circumnavigates a massive central pier which rises the full two storeys to form a stable base for the telescope in the dome above.

ADDRESS Madingley Road; 2.5 kilometres from the town centre
ACCESS none; visible from the grounds

John Clement Mead 1822–23

John Clement Mead 1822–23

The Pitt Building

During the early years of the nineteenth century the University Press, founded in 1534, was increasingly successful and rapidly developed its Silver Street site. James Walter's building of 1827 was followed shortly by Edward Blore's The Pitt Building on the Trumpington Street frontage. The Pitt Building was so named because it was paid for by excess funds from a collection raised to erect a statue to William Pitt in London's Hanover Square. Blore had a reputation for being an energetic, cheap and reliable architect and was known for his enthusiasm for the Tudor and Elizabethan styles, but a dull competence pervaded his work. The Pitt Press falls within his 'Tudor collegiate' genre, a revival of early Tudor-Gothic, and was probably the last, but certainly not the best, romantic university building to be built in Cambridge.

The building has a symmetrical principal façade to Trumpington Street composed of two identical three-storey ashlar ranges with a tall central entrance tower. The four-square tower has angle buttresses in three weathered stages ending in pinnacles, an entrance doorway flanked by tall niches with ogee heads, a distinctive oriel window lighting the Syndicate Meeting Room at first-floor level, and a pierced embattled parapet. The flanking ranges are set back and divided into three unequal bays by buttresses detailed as those on the tower. In the 1930s these ranges were completely remodelled internally and the fenestration was altered, thus changing their character.

ADDRESS Trumpington Street, at the corner of Silver Street
ACCESS none; visible from Trumpington Street

Edward Blore 1831–32

The University

Edward Blore 1831–32

Fitzwilliam Museum

In 1834 a competition was held for the design of a museum to house the Fitzwilliam bequest, a collection of paintings, etchings and books that had been left to the University in 1815. George Basevi's Greco-Roman design won over Rickman and Hussey's elaborate Gothic entry. Basevi was formerly a pupil of John Soane and by 1830 was established as one of the country's leading architects. The Fitzwilliam Museum is one of the major works of the early Victorian period and marks the transition from the pure neo-Greek style to a more baroque style which drew on both Roman and Greek precedents.

Basevi's impressive museum is a two-storey Portland stone block standing at the head of a monumental flight of steps, behind an extended loggia. The principal façade consists of a pedimented portico of eight giant Corinthian columns connected by similar colonnades to projecting solid pavilions at each side. There is a heavy entablature and cornice despite the museum being in a narrow street. However, the exaggerated modelling of the façade benefits the diagonal approach. The composition is self-assuredly axial and symmetrical on plan, with five galleries on each floor arranged around a central staircase hall. The carving of the capitals, frieze and main pediment was to designs by Charles Eastlake.

Basevi died in 1845 in an accident at Ely Cathedral and Charles R Cockerell took over the work, but in 1847 building was suspended due to lack of funds. Edward Middleton Barry resumed the work in 1870, the interior decoration of the staircase hall and galleries being his, and the museum was finally completed in 1875.

ADDRESS Trumpington Street
ACCESS open Tuesday to Saturday, 10.00–17.00; Sunday, 14.15–17.00

George Basevi 1835–45, C R Cockerell 1845–47, E M Barry 1870–75

George Basevi 1835–45, C R Cockerell 1845–47, E M Barry 1870–75

Selwyn Divinity School

Basil Champneys won the commission to design the Selwyn Divinity School in an architectural competition. Construction began shortly after the completion of his first building at Newnham College (see page 5.46), though there is here, appropriately perhaps, none of Newnham's light-hearted Queen Anne elegance. Although Champneys continues with the use of red brick, this time it is complemented by ashlar stone dressings. The style is early Tudor, and the details can be compared with King's College chapel (see page 5.36). Nonetheless, the building demonstrates Champney's skilful handling of plasticity, his use of decorative details such as the chequered parapet and his urban responsiveness in the way the corner turret echoes that of Anthony Salvin's 1859–68 Whewell's Court on the other side of All Saints' churchyard.

The main entrance opens into a vaulted cloister-like corridor behind the external buttresses. In the north part of the building are lecture rooms and a staircase leading to the main lecture room high in the central block. The cloister returns into the building to give access to the professors' rooms on the south side, and a further staircase that links them to the library above, and to the rostrum end of the main lecture room. The interior makes much use of exposed brickwork and dark timber, and is rather sombre.

Champneys also designed the elegant Gothic cross in the adjacent churchyard.

ADDRESS St John's Street
ACCESS none; visible from the street

Basil Champneys 1878–79

Basil Champneys 1878–79

University Library

Giles Gilbert Scott, grandson of the great Victorian architect George Gilbert Scott, shot to fame when in his early 20s he won the competition for the new Anglican cathedral in Liverpool.

The University Library, built some 30 years later, shares, with its massive tower, the monumentality of the earlier project. The prominent tower provides the axial termination for Scott's earlier Memorial Court for Clare College (see page 4.20), a Beaux-Arts gesture that seems particularly alien to the more domestic tradition of the colleges. This axis is now interrupted by Arup Associates' Clare College Library of 1984–86 (see page 4.22).

The tower contains book stacks lit by unbroken narrow windows, while wings extending to each side contain more book stacks. Beyond these are low pavilions housing reading rooms. The library is entered through a monumental arch, beyond which a staircase leads up to the catalogue room on the main level. This is flanked by two courtyards, and leads to the main reading room which lies across the rear of the building, but is now masked from outside by a substantial extension of the library to the west.

The details of the building are Italianate, emphasised by the use of narrow Roman bricks and a pantiled roof with eaves overhanging an attic storey. Yet, these seem at variance with the implied giant order created by the functional steel glazing of the book stack wings, a contrast in styles characteristic of much institutional English architecture of the 1930s.

ADDRESS between Burrell's Walk and West Road
ACCESS exhibition centre open Monday to Friday, 9.00–18.00; Saturday, 9.00–12.30

Giles Gilbert Scott 1931–34

The University

Giles Gilbert Scott 1931–34

Mond Laboratory

The 1930s were fallow times for modern architecture in Cambridge. Walter Gropius, exiled from the Bauhaus, briefly brushed with Cambridge, designing the Village College at Impington (see page 6.6) and an unbuilt extension for Christ's College (1936–37), before leaving for America. The Mond Laboratory together with Fen Court, Peterhouse (1939–40) and a few houses in Conduit Head Road (see page 1.16) were the only decent Modern Movement buildings built in Cambridge in the interwar period.

The building lies east of the Cavendish Laboratory and is rather unsatisfactorily located within the messy unplanned New Museums Site. It is unfortunate that the large scale and dull design of the surrounding buildings detract from the charming, almost naïve simplicity of Hughes' design. The composition of platonic solids consists of two rectangular wings joined by a rotunda to form an L-shaped building. The rotunda contains a double-height entrance area with a stair that wraps around the perimeter, and is a spatial delight. The 'modern' imagery is expressed in the elemental stripped-down form, the white sand–lime bricks that allude to concrete, the black-painted metal windows and the flat roofs. The crocodile carved into the brickwork to the right of the entrance as a tribute to Lord Rutherford who was nicknamed 'The Crocodile' is by Eric Gill. The nearby single-storey Workshop, also designed by Hughes, is contemporary with the Mond Laboratory and uses the same architectural vocabulary.

ADDRESS Department of Aerial Photography, New Museums Site, Pembroke Street
ACCESS entrance area and library open Monday to Thursday, 9.00–13.00, 14.00–17.00; Friday, 9.00–13.00, 14.00–16.00

H C Hughes 1932–33

H C Hughes 1932–33

School of Architecture extension

Colin St John Wilson set up a practice in Cambridge, independent of Leslie Martin, in 1956 and this project was one of his first commissions. The brief for the project was simple: to add a lecture room, criticism room, common room and tuition rooms to the rear of the existing accommodation, which was housed in the 1839 north end of Scroope Terrace. The result was a small building with a high theoretical content.

The building sits on the northern boundary facing the School's rear garden. A narrow glazed link connects the new building to the existing terrace and contains a staircase providing vertical circulation and making up the difference in floor levels between new and old. The building contains a lecture theatre and criticism space on the first floor, and tuition rooms and common room on the ground floor. What gives the building theoretical weight is that the ordering of the plan and elevations and the dimensional coordination accord with Le Corbusier's Modular proportioning system. The most powerful formal gesture is the acentric penetration of the building by the brick service core which acts as a symbolic axis mundi.

The Brutalist aesthetic – inspired particularly by Le Corbusier's Maisons Jaoul, at Neuilly-sur-Seine near Paris (1955–57) – which insists on an 'honest' display of the structure and materials of construction, makes this load-bearing brick and concrete building feel tough and primitive. This, together with the inventive and didactic detailing, from the cantilevered concrete staircase to the pivoted shutters of the lecture theatre roof-lights, makes the building seem highly appropriate for a school of architecture.

ADDRESS 1–5 Scroope Terrace, Trumpington Street
ACCESS none; visible from the side entrance lane

Colin St John Wilson and Alex Hardy 1957–58

Colin St John Wilson and Alex Hardy 1957–58

Faculty of Arts, Sidgwick Site

Hugh Casson won the commission for new buildings for the Arts Faculty in competition against Robert Atkinson. Casson's original scheme consisted of some 17 freestanding buildings loosely arranged to form a series of courts in a semi-formal manner characteristic of the 1950s Townscape movement. In the event only seven buildings, those closest to Sidgwick Avenue, were built according to Casson's design. The Faculties of English, Moral Sciences, Modern Languages and Mediaeval Languages inhabit a U-shaped block. Closing the west side of the 'U' to form a court is the long Faculty of Economics and Politics Building. Freestanding between the court and Sidgwick Avenue is Lady Mitchell Hall and to its east the Little Hall and lecture block (1958–60). Further east is the brick-built Faculty of Oriental Studies (1966–68).

Casson's architecture is representative of the 1950s New Empiricist style of which he was a great proponent. The U-shaped block is architecturally the most interesting. The accommodation is supported on a vast dark grey monolithic concrete underbelly raised on a double row of concrete pilotis to form a cloister at ground level. The upper storeys have walls of Portland stone cladding, penetrated by window openings whose sizes and positions relate to the function behind. A continuous clerestory of varying depth allows the flat roof to appear to float. The ground-level treatment alludes to Le Corbusier's Unité d'habitation at Marseilles (1947–52), but the translation is overpolite and it is this timidity that led to the chastisement of the New Empiricists by the Brutalists.

ADDRESS Sidgwick Avenue
ACCESS none; public external spaces open all hours

Casson Conder and Partners 1958–68

Casson Conder and Partners 1958–68

History Faculty

The History Faculty Building was the second of James Stirling's trium-virate of extraordinary Constructivist-inspired projects – after the Leicester Engineering Building (1959–63) and before the Florey Building, Oxford (1966–71). All three buildings have proved controversial, attracting justified criticism from their users for the lack of environmental control and constructional faults but praise from architects for their radical inventiveness of form and tectonic daring. Stirling won the commission for a new History Faculty in a limited competition and the building seen today is very similar to the original design except that a change of site, to a more central location on the Sidgwick Site, resulted in its rotation through 90 degrees.

The building houses a library, teaching spaces, offices and common rooms. Stirling ignored the college library precedents in Cambridge and based his design on a kind of sculptural accretion in which each typo-logical element was given a distinct form. Thus the red tile and patent glazed L-shaped block contains the cellular teaching spaces, while the quadrant under a cascading steel and glass roof contains the reading room and book stacks. The understated main entrance in the north-west corner opens directly to the enquiry desk, catalogue area and major vertical circulation towers. Beyond and one metre below is the vast Reading Room bounded by two levels of shelving units fanning radially on sight lines from the enquiry desk. The form has been likened to a quadrant of a Bentham panoptican and to an open book. Eclectic references to nine-teenth- and twentieth-century architecture abound.

ADDRESS Sidgwick Site, between West Road and Sidgwick Avenue
ACCESS none; visible from the Sidgwick Site

James Stirling 1964–66

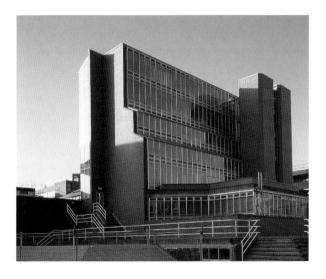

James Stirling 1964–66

University Centre

The University Centre was commissioned to provide social facilities for graduate members of the University. The architects, second-generation modernists, organised the complex programme of dining hall, common rooms, bars and other ancillary accommodation by juxtaposing a series of distinct and strongly articulated parts, each part an 'ideal' response to the programme. The result is a series of contiguous canted pavilions wrapping around three sides of the dining hall pavilion, with the zone between the two structural systems taken up by horizontal circulation.

The main elevation clearly demonstrates that it is made up of four stone-clad pavilions sitting on an engineering brick base. The roach-bed Portland stone cladding panels with their open joins, expressed fixings and lead-clad strip windows have a distinctive *art brut* flavour. The entrance is marked rather unsuccessfully at the parting of the end pavilions by a concrete lift tower. Inside, an internal corridor at each level gives access to the smaller rooms facing the River Cam and an elegant top-lit concrete stair with memorable lead-clad treads leads one effortlessly to the top-floor dining hall. This double-height space has an impressive clear-span timber roof with tie-rods that spring across the diagonal. The aesthetic is based throughout on the assertive and direct expression of the materials (concrete, stone, oak, lead) and constructional techniques (concrete frame and infill). The language is clearly of Brutalist origin and gives the building its characteristic toughness. However, the inventiveness and quality of the detailing creates a curiously luxurious atmosphere.

ADDRESS Granta Place
ACCESS apply at reception

Howell Killick Partridge and Amis 1963–67

Howell Killick Partridge and Amis 1963–67

Kettle's Yard

Kettle's Yard was a row of four derelict artisans' cottages when it was bought by Jim and Helen Ede in 1956 and made into their home. In *A Way of Life: Kettle's Yard* (1984) Jim Ede describes the calm environment of neutral tones, natural materials and found objects he created there as a setting for his collection of early twentieth-century paintings and sculpture.

In 1966 Ede persuaded Cambridge University to accept Kettle's Yard, the collection and a generous endowment as a gift, and in 1970 the extension to the house that he had worked hard to see built was opened. Martin and Owers' extension is entered from the first floor of the original house. Skilfully, they continued the domestic scale and intimate spaces of the house in a modern idiom, while doubling its size and providing a space large enough for concerts to take place. Internally the walls are rendered and painted white, and are naturally lit from continuous roof-lights. An exhibition gallery was added as a second phase. This has its own entrance from a small courtyard north of the house, overlooking the medieval remains of St Peter's Church and churchyard. Externally the building is of Cambridge stock brick and dark stained boarding, its plain walls, which support a flat roof, relating well to their surroundings.

Brown Bland and Cole's extension of the gallery into the ground floor of the buildings in Castle Street continues the gallery's sequence of modest top-lit spaces, while giving it a glazed street frontage and a visual link with the outside world.

ADDRESS Kettle's Yard, between Northampton Street and Castle Street
ACCESS house open Tuesday to Sunday, 13.30–16.30 (winter 14.00–16.00); gallery open Tuesday to Sunday, 12.30–17.30; open Bank Holiday Mondays

Leslie Martin and David Owers 1969–70, Brown Bland and Cole 1994

Leslie Martin and David Owers 1969–70, Brown Bland and Cole

New Museums Building

Twentieth-century expansion of the University's science faculties took place within the urban block contained by Corn Exchange Street, Downing Street, Free School Lane and Bene't Street known as the New Museums Site. One of the series of badly coordinated buildings to be built on this site was a building to house the Departments of Zoology, Metallurgy and Computer Technology, and the University Museum of Zoology.

The building lies uncomfortably out of alignment with Corn Exchange Street but orthogonal with the other boundaries of the urban block. It appears as a huge technological megastructure; an incomprehensible collection of lead-clad towers, monumental concrete frames and suspended units of accommodation. One is reminded of the drawings of the Russian Constructivists. However, it is more likely that the inspiration came more directly from the contemporary university work of Lyons, Israel and Ellis. Although the complex sits very badly on its site and is almost impossible to enter, the building's organisation is in itself quite rational. Two parallel ranges of laboratories are linked at regular intervals by horizontal circulation routes to form a series of internal courtyards. Offices are contained in the two separately expressed lead-clad towers, which are linked to the main body of the building by glazed staircases. The Museum of Zoology is at the northern end of the megastructure and contains some good internal spaces. A tough architectural language is employed here with confidence and dexterity and it represents a period when the internal rationale for the building and its direct architectural expression was far more important than its response to context.

ADDRESS Corn Exchange Street
ACCESS Museum of Zoology open Monday to Friday, 14.00–16.30

Arup Associates 1964–71

Arup Associates 1964–71

Cambridge Crystallographic Data Centre

In the early 1960s the Danish architect Erik Sørensen had designed a house in Cambridge at 8a Hills Avenue for Professor Olga Kennard. Kennard became Scientific Director of the Cambridge Crystallographic Data Centre, and she was Sørensen's client and patron for the centre's new building.

By joining his building to the rear of Easton and Robertson's 1953–60 Chemistry Department and providing a street frontage opposite a 1960s' multistorey car park, Sørensen attempted to heal some of the damage that these two interlopers had caused to Newtown, an attractive early-Victorian residential part of Cambridge. The street elevation, of thin hand-made Danish red brickwork, is a studied exercise in layering a thick wall. The small windows have grey granite reveals, while a discontinuous cornice and sills in stone are used as ordering devices. Alongside the entrance a crystalline form in flint refers to the building's use, while full-height mirrored recesses terminate the wall ends.

The red brickwork and other quotations from the façade continue inside the building. The open-plan research areas on the top two floors are accessed by a glass lift, and are lit by a tall curving roof-light that channels light into the heart of the building. On the roof is a lunchroom and small terrace. The ground floor houses the reception area, the database and secretarial accommodation, and is partly raised to allow light into the basement research laboratory.

ADDRESS Union Road
ACCESS none; visible from the street

Zibrandtsen Architects (Erik Sørensen) 1991–92

Zibrandtsen Architects (Erik Sørensen) 1991–92

Judge Institute of Management Studies

This is without doubt the most colourful and individualistic modern building in Cambridge.

On Trumpington Street John Outram restored the polychromy to the old Addenbroke's Hospital ward block, and crowned the weak 1920s' top floor with a strong cornice and pediment. Behind the ward block, which now houses the library, computer laboratory and seminar rooms, he built a new 'Gallery'. This tall atrium is the building's main circulation space, containing galleries and criss-crossing staircases. A riot of colour (though not to Outram's preferred decorative scheme), the Gallery is articulated by a system of monumental columns and beams which contain structure, services and service maintenance access. These Outram has christened the 'Robot Order', and he uses them both to free himself of the need for suspended ceilings, and to create 'Big architecture'. The Gallery leads to 'The Ark' and 'The Castle', newly built blocks facing Tennis Court Road. The four-storey Ark block, placed axially behind the ward block, contains tutorial offices with a roof garden above, while to its south the Castle block has service areas on the ground floor, with lecture rooms above.

Outram sees the building's physical organisation as a metaphor for the Greek city, or polis, and the Gallery as the 'Acropolis Temple'. His development (with Techrete of Dublin) of two-colour inlaid concrete, concrete with crushed brick and marble aggregate, and lacquer-glazed black aggregate concrete for the capitals allows colour to infuse the whole scheme. 'Colour', says Outram, 'is pure idea, pure intellectuality, pure emotion.'

ADDRESS Trumpington Street
ACCESS none; visible from Trumpington Street and Tennis Court Road

John Outram 1995

The University

John Outram 1995

Law Faculty

Sir Norman Foster's new building for the Law Faculty has made a bold attempt to respond to the other buildings on the Sidgwick Site, and to reinforce the north–south pedestrian route, while employing an uncompromisingly high-tech style. The form of the building externally is a half cylinder laid across the site, with the southern wall, which faces Casson Conder's buildings, sliced vertically and clad in a matching stone. The north wall takes the form of a huge curving glass roof, supported by a triangulated Vierendeel steel structure, which sweeps down to meet the ground. The extrusion is cut off at an angle at the west end in response to the angled façade of James Stirling's History Faculty Building (see page 3.24) and this, together with a slender steel column, marks the entrance. The junction of the glass skin of the end wall with the curving roof challenges the pre-eminence of the curving roof and is arguably the least satisfactory detail in the building.

The teaching rooms are on the lower-ground and ground floors, and the book stacks and reading spaces are three decks above. The decks are held back from the curved glass roof to form a dramatic atrium which unites the entrance with all levels of the building (and as a result creates an unfortunate noise attenuation problem). Within the envelope the usual Foster discipline and rigour are present, resulting in a series of ethereal spaces with immaculate mechanistic detailing. One looks forward to his future buildings for the English and Criminology Faculties on the adjacent site.

ADDRESS Sidgwick Site, West Road
ACCESS none; visible from the Sidgwick Site

Sir Norman Foster and Partners 1995

The University

Sir Norman Foster and Partners 1995

Colleges to the north of King's College Chapel

Christ's College, Entrance Court

Christ's College was refounded by Lady Margaret Beaufort in 1505, and new buildings were built between 1505 and 1511 on the site of its earlier foundation. The gatehouse facing St Andrew's Street, although refaced by Robert Grumbold in 1714, largely retains its early sixteenth-century appearance, with octagonal turrets on the corners and a four-centred archway containing late sixteenth-century oak doors. Above the archway, on an ogee-shaped label, are the arms of Lady Margaret supported by two yales, fabulous heraldic beasts.

The inside of the two-storey court, including the gatehouse, was refaced in a simple classical style using ashlar stonework under the direction of James Essex from 1758 to 1769. Essex introduced pedimented doorways and regularly spaced sash windows, with a grander window in the Venetian style in the gatehouse. Fortunately, he retained one original oriel window above the entrance to the Master's Lodge on the east side. To its left he emphasised the entrance to the antechapel by giving it a symmetrical treatment, with a larger doorway and a tall parapet with blind windows. The interior of the chapel was refitted in 1702–03, while the early sixteenth-century open timber roof was again revealed by the removal of a later plaster ceiling in the nineteenth century.

The hall, in the south-east corner of the court, was taken down and rebuilt in the original Tudor style, using the original ground plan by George Gilbert Scott in 1876–79. Scott not only adapted and reused the sixteenth-century timber roof, but also reused an eighteenth-century cupola. Later in the nineteenth century the library, south of the gatehouse, was extended further south and given Tudor windows by George Bodley.

ADDRESS St Andrew's Street
ACCESS college open daily, 9.30–14.00; closed May and June

1505–11, refaced by James Essex 1758–69

1505–11, refaced by James Essex 1758–69

Christ's College, Fellows' Building

The period before the Civil War was one of expansion for Christ's College, and the Fellows' Building was built to relieve pressure on space. It stands alone some distance east of the Entrance Court (see page 4.2). Although for its time the Fellows' Building is somewhat dated, it is the most architecturally accomplished mid-seventeenth-century building in Cambridge. Unfortunately, the designer's name is not recorded.

The building, of ashlar-faced stone, has three storeys and an attic, and is 11 bays wide. The bays are divided into groups of three by prominent lead down-pipes, and the block is framed at each end by a half bay of plain walling with Ionic corner pilasters. The end elevations have the same architectural treatment as the two fronts. Internally, the two oak staircases are original, each serving a pair of sets of rooms on each floor.

The various elements of the façade are rhythmically articulated. The ground floor has three pedimented doorways, between which are block-rusticated windows. The central doorway is flanked by pilasters supporting a triangular pediment, and has a wider four-centred arch leading to the Fellows' Garden. The prominent first-floor windows have stone mullion-and-transom crosses (here used for the first time in Cambridge) with shallow pediments where they occur above each doorway. There is a further storey of crossed windows. The parapet has diagonal balusters in front of each dormer window, with a semicircular cresting reminiscent of the Jacobean period on the solid panels between. The dormers above the doorways have semicircular pediments; the others are triangular.

ADDRESS St Andrew's Street
ACCESS college open daily, 9.30–16.00; closed May and June

1640–44

1640–44

Christ's College, New Court

Denys Lasdun was asked by the college to produce a development plan for the northern edge of the college grounds, between the Fellows' Garden and King Street. The scheme was to contain student rooms with associated facilities.

What is seen today is the first phase of a scheme which would have repeated in a gentle arc along the full length of the King Street boundary. The fragment built has an enormous impact when approached from Third Court. A series of terraces steps back from a wing of communal rooms at garden level to form a huge boundary wall to the college. The elemental nature of the precast concrete constructional kit determines the appearance of the building; the width of the student rooms determines the module. This divides the vast wall into smaller repeated units and arguably makes the building seem more human, like an inhabited cascade. The stepped section allows each student room to face south, and to open out onto a terrace over the student room below. Staircases step up through the section of the building, leading to rather dark internal corridors from which the rooms are accessed.

There were shops facing King Street and service areas under the building, but this area was subsequently filled in with additional student rooms to a more traditional design by Architects Design Partnership. The incredible single-mindedness of the megastructure concept is breathtaking. However, in the end one feels that the building is tyrannised by its own internal logic and that too many sacrifices, both contextually and functionally, are made to justify the grand gesture.

ADDRESS St Andrew's Street, King Street
ACCESS college open daily, 9.30–16.00; closed May and June

Denys Lasdun and Partners 1966–70

Denys Lasdun and Partners 1966–70

Churchill College

Sheppard Robson won the competition for the first post-war Cambridge college against some of the leading architects of the day, including Alison and Peter Smithson, and Stirling and Gowan. The idea of building a twentieth-century version of the Cambridge court typology probably won them the competition.

The complex consists of an entrance block adjacent to Storey's Way containing communal facilities, ten interlinked residential courts in three groups, with a compound of Fellows' housing (see page 4.10) and a chapel at the far west end of the site. The accommodation is organised about a ceremonial axis that links the monumental entrance gateway and Porter's Lodge to the communal rooms. From this axial route covered walkways lead to the freestanding library and the groups of residential courts. Ground-floor cloisters provide access to staircases to the student rooms, which are arranged in groups, again following the collegiate tradition.

Anyone approaching the college might be forgiven for regarding the architecture as dull and monotonous. The three-storey brick residential ranges with expressed concrete floor bands and bay windows exhibit a Brutalist aesthetic. Significant variation occurs only in the design of the first-floor hall with its monumental concrete vaulted roof, and the library. However, despite the rather relentless consistency of the architectural language the scale of the elements is well judged, and there is just enough variation to prevent disorientation. The addition of works of art liberally placed throughout the college provides relief and delight.

ADDRESS Storey's Way, off Madingley Road
ACCESS apply at porter's lodge

Sheppard Robson and Partners 1958–65

Sheppard Robson and Partners 1958–65

Churchill College, Fellows' Housing

This group of Fellows' flats was the first of the new college buildings to be built. They stand as an isolated block in the north-west corner of the site. The development is a complex accretion of 20 identical flat plans, 12 on the ground floor and eight on the first floor, which are stacked and rotated so that each flat is indecipherable from the whole. In fact, each flat has a separate entrance (the ground-floor flats via a walled forecourt; the upper flats up an external stair) and a private outlook: a small enclosed garden for the ground-floor flats and a roof-terrace for the first-floor flats.

The architectural language employed is a variation on the style of the main college buildings (see page 4.8). Load-bearing brick walls laid out with a strict orthogonal geometry, expressed concrete floor slabs, timber windows filling cut-outs in the wall plane and floating roofs with copper fascias are deployed with a rigorous Brutalist discipline, namely the display of the constructional technique and the 'honest' use of materials. The complex has many of the failings inherent in Brutalism, such as a lack of formal hierarchy and absence of colour or humour, yet it remains a fine example of the genre.

ADDRESS Storey's Way, off Madingley Road
ACCESS apply at porter's lodge

Sheppard Robson and Partners 1959–60

Sheppard Robson and Partners 1959–60

Churchill College, Møller Centre

The Møller Centre is a residential training centre for business and industry commissioned by Churchill College as a commercial venture. The new building houses conference facilities, and includes 71 bedrooms.

The building has a strong simple form: a long three-storey banded brick block with an octagonal tower on the south side, with a square vaulted lecture theatre and a second short block on the north side. The tower faces Churchill's playing fields and stands out like a beacon when seen from Madingley Road. It houses the dining and reception rooms for the centre, and the linear block contains the bedrooms. The entrance, on the other side of the building, is marked by a projecting canopy that sets up a 45-degree axis through the main block, terminated by the tower. The play of geometries and platonic forms can best be understood from the reception space, which is one of the most successful architectural spaces in the building (together with the dramatic tower). The linear block is sliced at 45 degrees at the east end, pierced by a double-height through route, and contains a single-loaded corridor with the rooms facing the playing fields. The most contentious aspect of the building is its architectural aesthetic. It is difficult to understand the allusion in this context to a vocabulary inspired by the Italian rationalist architect Aldo Rossi. Neither the typological nor the linguistic precedents so important to Rossi's theory, as laid out in his *The Architecture of the City* (1966), seem appropriate or relevant here. Additionally, the rather insubstantial detailing does nothing to convince the visitor that this is a building of quality.

ADDRESS Storey's Way, off Madingley Road
ACCESS apply at reception

Henning Larsen 1992

Henning Larsen 1992

Clare College, Old Court

In 1638 Clare College started replacing its medieval court with one almost twice the size. By 1642, when the Civil War brought work to a halt, the east and south ranges, built and probably designed by master mason John Westley, were complete. Work was resumed in earnest in 1669 with the range facing the river, although the gateway and Master's Lodge at the north end were only completed in 1707. The north range was meanwhile built in 1683–93. Both were built and designed by master mason Robert Grumbold.

The buildings, of three storeys, with basements and an attic, appear remarkably homogeneous. This is thanks to a coherent master-plan, the same building height and window module throughout, and the use of identical stone. However, a development in architectural styles is clearly apparent. The west gateway, with its fan vault, ogee-headed niches, oriel windows, block-rusticated columns and elaborate top storey, is a mixture of late-Gothic and early-Renaissance motifs. The windows in the east and south ranges originally had Tudor four-centred arches, but these were replaced with flat heads in 1762 when the parapet battlements were replaced with the present balustrade.

By contrast, the two-storey north range containing the hall and kitchens, with the Combination Room and library above, has carefully handled wall planes, and windows with mullion-and-transom crosses. The west elevation facing the river has a giant Order of Ionic pilasters and first-floor windows heavily emphasised with pediments and keystones. Some windows originally had crosses too, but in 1719 these were given sashes, which were lengthened in 1815.

ADDRESS Trinity Lane
ACCESS college open daily, 10.00–16.30; closed May and June; admission charge April to September

John Westley 1638–42, Robert Grumbold 1669–1707

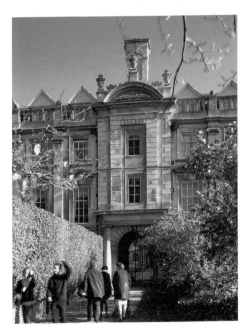

Colleges to the north of King's College Chapel

John Westley 1638–42, Robert Grumbold 1669–1707

Clare College, Bridge

Clare College built its bridge to give access to Butt Close, a piece of land west of the river acquired as part of a land swap with King's College in 1638. This land deal also allowed rebuilding of Old Court (see page 4.14) to start and, despite their contrasting styles, the east range of Old Court and the bridge are contemporary. The bridge may have been needed to provide access for building materials.

Clare Bridge, just one of many fine college bridges spanning the River Cam, was the first to be built in the classical style. Thomas Grumbold, the first of a family of Northamptonshire master masons to settle in Cambridge, provided the college with a design, and also constructed the bridge. It has three segmental spans with triangular cutwaters between. The taller central arch has a level balustrade, now charmingly dipping in the middle, while the balustrade to the flanking arches slopes up towards the centre. The square balusters are arranged diagonally, and heavy stone balls are positioned regularly along the coping. The die stones between the balusters are embellished with watery subjects such as sea horses, rocks, shells, river creatures and a triton.

The bridge is approached by contemporary causeways, that to the west being enclosed by a fine triple gateway of wrought iron of 1714.

ADDRESS Trinity Lane
ACCESS college open daily, 10.00–16.30; closed May and June; admission charge April to September

Thomas Grumbold (master mason) 1638–40

Thomas Grumbold (master mason) 1638–40

Clare College, Chapel

Some 50 years after the completion of Old Court (see page 4.14), Clare College continued its rebuilding programme with a new chapel and library on the site occupied by its early sixteenth-century chapel and library. The architect was James Burrough, Master of Caius College and an amateur architect, and the builder was James Essex, who completed the work after Burrough's death in 1764.

The chapel is reached through a doorway with a shell hood of 1685 in the north-east corner of Old Court. This leads to an access passage, which was remodelled when the chapel was built. The elegant antechapel is, uniquely, octagonal on plan, and is lit from above by a domed cupola. The chapel, which is raised above an undercroft, is entered under a gallery containing a modern organ. The oak gallery, pews, panelling and pedimented altarpiece are original, as is the delicate elliptical plastered vault, the elliptical apse at the east end and the black-and-white marble floor.

Externally, Corinthian pilasters separate five bays of arched windows. These are raised on a rusticated plinth containing windows to the undercroft, and are terminated by pairs of pilasters flanking blind panels. The cornice and balustrade continue the same line as the rest of Old Court. The arrangement of blind arched window, flanking pilasters and pediment at the east end recalls the west end of Christopher Wren's chapel for Pembroke College (see page 5.56), built a century earlier.

ADDRESS Trinity Lane
ACCESS college open daily, 10.00–16.30; closed May and June; admission charge April to September

James Burrough and James Essex 1763–69

Colleges to the north of King's College Chapel

James Burrough and James Essex 1763–69

Clare College, Memorial Court

Memorial Court was built to accommodate increased student numbers, and to commemorate those members of the college who fell in the First World War. Clare was the first college to take the radical decision, much criticised at the time, to build beyond The Backs, to the west of Queen's Road, a decision subsequently followed by other colleges.

In building a court with sets of rooms accessed off staircases, Giles Gilbert Scott followed the Cambridge tradition. His court was, however, extended to the west by two parallel blocks and left open on that side. Nine years later, Scott began his University Library (see page 3.16), providing a grandiose stop to the axis set up by Memorial Court. In 1953–55 he added a further court, Thirkill Court, south of Memorial Court. More recently, a new college library (see page 4.22) has been constructed across the court, dividing it into two parts.

Scott worked in a restrained neo-Georgian style, using Adamesque Grecian details such as the funerary urns which adorn the triumphal arch at the entrance, and the motif of slender Corinthian columns used in pairs to define the major openings. The court is of two storeys, with a third storey added to the principal elevations. It is of pale grey brickwork with elongated quoins, and timber windows set flush in the wall plane. Portland stone is used for the plinth, cornice and other architectural details.

ADDRESS Queen's Road
ACCESS apply at porter's lodge, Memorial Court

Giles Gilbert Scott 1922–35

Giles Gilbert Scott 1922–35

Clare College, Library

Clare College approached Philip Dowson, an alumnus of the college, to design a new library and music rooms. The tiny building that resulted caused much controversy at the time because of its interruption of the visual axis linking the main gateway of Giles Gilbert Scott's Memorial Court (see page 4.20) to the tower of his University Library (see page 3.16). Dowson argued that the building would reduce the overpowering effect of the axis and give the residential court a more human scale.

However, the library appears not to know if it is an object sitting in space or the west range of the court. This is particularly apparent from the college side where the octagonal apse of the library slavishly copies the materials and details of the existing neo-Georgian ranges to which it is joined with wings. The entrance elevation, inspired by Filippo Brunelleschi's Pazzi Chapel in S Croce, Florence (c.1430), faces the University Library rather than the college. It is difficult to know whether this was the right orientation, or indeed whether the building's imagery and low proportions are appropriate to the setting.

Internally the building is more successful. A small double-height octagonal entrance hall, appropriately alluding to the college's eighteenth-century antechapel (see page 4.18), gives access to the music rooms housed in the two-storey front range and the galleried library in the octagonal apse at the rear. Although the plan is disciplined by the radiating geometry of the octagonal lobby, the spaces are remarkably usable, and careful lighting and attention to detail provide a feeling of quality as well as utility.

ADDRESS Memorial Court, The Backs
ACCESS none; visible from Memorial Court; apply at porter's lodge

Philip Dowson, Arup Associates 1984–86

Colleges to the north of King's College Chapel

Philip Dowson, Arup Associates 1984–86

Fitzwilliam College

Fitzwilliam House was founded as an 'approved society' in 1889. Its foundation as a college came in 1958 when it moved from Trumpington Street to its current site. Unlike other colleges Fitzwilliam had no endowment and the incremental nature of the government finance influenced Denys Lasdun's master-plan. The concept was to build a nucleus of communal facilities, forming the 'heart' of the college, followed by a series of linked residential ranges expanding in a spiral form, the college thus seeming complete at every stage. It was envisaged that the final form, a vast court, would have as its twin foci the communal block and an existing early nineteenth-century house. In the event only about one-half of the master-plan was built before it was abandoned in 1990.

Fitzwilliam is not one of Lasdun's best buildings. His earlier Royal College of Physicians, London (1959–61), and later residences for Christ's College (see page 4.6) are both more rigorous and inventive. The architectural language of Fitzwilliam seems to reflect the austerity of the funding rather too successfully. The three-storey, dark engineering brick residential ranges with their alternating piers and glazed slots running between expressed concrete floor slabs are dull and monotonous. The allusion to monastic architecture or to Le Corbusier's Monastery of La Tourette (1957–60) is made in a rather uninspired manner. The focus of the college is the hall. This signals its presence with a large rooftop lantern, which has a series of white concrete parabolic arches, but a flat, diagonally coffered ceiling inside. It is an example of 1950s British Empiricism, which at the time was much criticised for its picturesque effect and lack of discipline.

ADDRESS Huntingdon Road, Storey's Way
ACCESS apply at porter's lodge

Denys Lasdun and Partners 1958–67

Denys Lasdun and Partners 1958–67

Fitzwilliam College, New Court

Denys Lasdun's master-plan for Fitzwilliam College (see page 4.24), which suggested a spiral growth of the earlier blocks, was abandoned by MacCormac Jamieson Prichard and Wright when they were commissioned to design 200-odd new student rooms. They suggested that future development should create a series of linked courts. New Court is the first phase of the plan and comprises 85 undergraduate study-bedrooms. The accommodation is arranged in four staircases in an L-shaped block abutting the end of one of Lasdun's ranges, thus creating a three-sided court. The façades of the new building respond to Lasdun's buildings by continuing his floor heights and building height, and by the use of the same engineering bricks, but this is no slavish copy. Beneath a floating roof, white precast concrete posts and beams modulate the façade into a series of bays that step in and out, incorporating corner bay windows. The effect is lighter and less severe than the earlier buildings.

Inside, the playful common staircases make up for the polite restraint of the elevations. Each of the 'houses' is entered under the communal first-floor kitchen, which acts as a lookout. The staircases begin as a straight flight to first-floor level where they divide into two flights running in opposite directions along the spine of the building. The enjoyment of the Escher-like journey upwards is enhanced by roof-lights and by the use of broad horizontal bands of grey-stained ash veneer for the staircase walls. The architects' familiar Mackintosh-inspired square motif is deployed liberally for the internal fittings, and the overall effect is rich and playful.

ADDRESS Huntingdon Road, or Storey's Way
ACCESS apply at porter's lodge

MacCormac Jamieson Prichard and Wright 1985

Colleges to the north of King's College Chapel

MacCormac Jamieson Prichard and Wright 1985

Fitzwilliam College, Chapel

Following the architects' commission for New Court (see page 4.26), MacCormac Jamieson Prichard and Wright were asked to build a new chapel. Externally it reads as a monumental cylinder, somewhat reminiscent of the Swiss architect Mario Botta's work. The blank façades of the cylinder continue the string courses and parapet lines of the adjoining buildings. Yet the formal quality of the cylinder suggests that it contains something special. The fact that the cylinder is incomplete is not apparent from the major pedestrian approaches: that treat awaits.

The entrance is from a passage between old and new. At ground level there is a low crypt, suitably dark and contemplative. Two staircases follow the curve of the external walls to the main chapel on the first floor, an upward passage towards the light which is appropriately spiritual. Within the circular double-height space of the chapel, a vast bay window, an altar, a lower-roofed seating area and an organ located above the passage create the directionality deemed necessary for religious services. The large window sitting in the opening in the parted cylinder is remarkably powerful. Such an expansive view of the garden has the effect of reconnecting man with nature. Great care has been taken with the detailing of the internal finishes and the specially designed oak furniture and fittings.

The total effect is masterly: firmness, commodity and delight are all satisfied and provide a fitting setting for worship or contemplation.

ADDRESS Huntingdon Road, or Storey's Way
ACCESS apply at porter's lodge

MacCormac Jamieson Prichard and Wright 1990

Fitzwilliam College, Chapel

MacCormac Jamieson Prichard and Wright 1990

Girton College

When Emily Davies was persuaded to relocate the college for women that she had founded in Hitchin, she chose, for the sake of propriety, a site outside Cambridge near Girton village. She chose Alfred Waterhouse as the architect.

Waterhouse was active both at Oxford and Cambridge, having worked in Cambridge at Gonville and Caius (see page 4.40), Pembroke (see page 5.58) and Jesus Colleges. Unlike Basil Champneys' lyrical designs for Newnham College (see page 5.46), the other Victorian women's college, Waterhouse worked in a no-nonsense Gothic, using machine-made red roof tiles, hard red bricks and terracotta, and white-painted windows and dormers. His buildings, added piecemeal as funds allowed, have a business-like, almost institutional quality, an aspect not helped by the use of long access corridors in place of the usual Cambridge staircases. Only the introduction of gables, a circular staircase tower and the gate tower added in 1887 alleviate this.

In 1899–1902 Paul Waterhouse, who had become his father's partner in 1891, continued the work in the same materials, though in a somewhat more Tudor style, adding the chapel and Chapel Wing, the hall, and Woodlands Wing. It was Michael Waterhouse, the third generation of the same family, who, in completing Woodlands Court in 1931–32 with Giles Gilbert Scott (grandson of George Gilbert Scott, another Victorian architect) as consultant, finally broke the mould. His use of dark roof tiles, a brownish coloured brick, beige terracotta dressings around the windows and an abstracted style with Tudor references results in a less strident appearance.

ADDRESS Huntingdon Road
ACCESS apply at porter's lodge

Alfred Waterhouse 1872–87, Paul Waterhouse 1899–1902

Michael Waterhouse 1995–97

Gonville and Caius College, Caius Court

The Renaissance polymath Dr John Caius studied medicine with Vesalius in Padua, travelled in Italy and France, and became Royal Physician before dedicating his riches to Gonville Hall, where he became co-founder, and Master in 1559.

The new court he gave the college consisted of two stone ranges of two storeys with attics, closed to the north by the existing chapel, but left open to the south to allow for ventilation. Overlaying these medieval buildings was a programme of gates and towers that explored the new Renaissance style described in Sebastiano Serlio's *Five Books of Architecture* (1537) and in England by John Shute's *First and Chief Groundes of Architecture* (1563), and witnessed first-hand by Caius during his travels abroad.

The Gate of Humility, removed to the Master's Garden in 1868, provided a new entrance to the college from Trinity Street. The student then approached the Gate of Virtue along a tree-lined walk. This gate has three storeys of superimposed orders and a pedimented attic. Inside the court it is marked by a hexagonal tower with an ogival dome. The Gate of Honour established a new axis linking a new passage from the original Gonville Court (see page 4.34) with Schools Lane, the route that graduating students would follow to the Schools Building (see page 3.2). This gate is a miniature essay of three storeys in Renaissance detail.

Caius also built tall, octagonal stair towers on the south side of the chapel and the Master's Lodge, and erected a column supporting 60 sundials in the court, all now removed. Theodore Haveus of Cleve in Germany completed the column after Caius's death in 1573.

ADDRESS Trinity Street
ACCESS college open daily, 9.00–14.00; closed May and June

Dr John Caius 1565–75

Colleges to the north of King's College Chapel

Dr John Caius 1565–75

4.34

Gonville and Caius College, Gonville Court and Chapel

Gonville Court was the original part of Gonville and Caius College. It was built starting in 1353 by the executor of Edmund Gonville, the first founder of the college, and completed c.1490. The original entrance was from Trinity Lane to the north, the hall and library were in the west range and the Master's Lodge was in the angle between the west range and the chapel, which stood where it is now. The present small court gives a good idea of the size and height of the original, but it was entirely refaced or rebuilt in the eighteenth century and later, after the construction in 1565–73 of Caius Court (see page 4.32) to the south.

James Burrough, Bursar of the college and Master from 1754, was the amateur architect who designed the new work. In 1751–55 the east and west ranges were refaced, and the north range rebuilt. Burrough used ashlar stonework with parapets for the walls, regularly spaced and well-proportioned sash windows, and pedimented dormers to give the court a uniform classical appearance. The cupola on the west range had previously been added in 1728 to designs by James Essex. Subsequently, the west range was remodelled internally and paired doorways added by Anthony Salvin in 1853, with an oriel window added in 1878. The east range was rebuilt behind its façade in 1868–70 by Alfred Waterhouse.

The medieval chapel had been aligned along a lane on its south side. In 1637 it was extended to the east and a five-sided wood-panelled ceiling was added. In 1718–26 the exterior was refaced, and in 1870 the apsidal east end was added to designs by Waterhouse. Notable inside is a 1575 monument to Dr Caius by Theodore Haveus of Cleve.

ADDRESS Trinity Street
ACCESS college open daily, 9.00–14.00; closed May and June

James Burrough 1751–55

Gonville and Caius College, Gonville Court and Chapel

Colleges to the north of King's College Chapel

James Burrough 1751–55

Gonville and Caius College, Library

The monumental building which is seen today is merely the north range of a vast classical quadrangle that Charles Robert Cockerell designed to house the university's growing collection of books formerly housed in the Old Schools (see page 3.2). Cockerell won the scheme by competition in 1829, and the foundation stone was laid in 1837. His University Library is a remarkable intellectual and personal exercise in neo-classical design, and confirms his status as one of the best architects of the first half of the nineteenth century.

The east end, in Portland stone, uses the triumphal arch motif to mark the entrance. Colossal pilasters support a heavy entablature surmounted by a deep rusticated attic. The centre is pierced by a deeply recessed arch, containing the entrance, with a semicircular window and balcony above. The other elevations of the library, in red-brown Whitby stone, concede nothing to the narrowness of the setting. The north elevation, to Senate House Passage, has seven bays with first-floor pilasters and half-round attic windows, terminated by solid end bays supporting arched chimney stacks, while the courtyard elevation has giant pilasters.

Inside are libraries on two levels. The principal level, a splendid high tunnel-vaulted volume, criss-crossed with heavy ribs, is flanked by seven side-niches for bookcases. These have transverse tunnel vaults and large arch-headed windows, with galleries above. Ionic screens terminate the linear space, which has Roman grandeur. Stairs from the entrance block lead to both the basement vaults and the upper-floor galleries. The building now houses the library of Gonville and Caius College.

ADDRESS north of Old Schools and west of Senate House
ACCESS none; visible from Senate House Passage

Charles Robert Cockerell 1837–40

Charles Robert Cockerell 1837–40

Gonville and Caius College, Hall

The floor of the original fourteenth-century hall in the west range of Gonville Court was raised in 1589 to provide space underneath for cellars and a buttery. In 1792 the hall's interior was remodelled by John Soane, who installed an elegant plaster coffered segmental vault beneath the medieval open timber roof, and a semicircular window and arched screen at the north end.

However, Soane's work was swept away in 1853–54 when Anthony Salvin added a new hall, library and extension to the Master's Lodge in the yards between the west range and Trinity Lane. The new block, which is scarcely visible from inside the college, towers above Trinity Lane. Salvin used red brick with stone dressings, and his late-Tudor style, with tall windows, buttresses, curving Dutch gables and brick diaper patterning, is somewhat reminiscent of the royal palace at Hampton Court, Middlesex. Access is from Gonville Court through a double doorway and entrance hall leading to two opposed transverse stairways.

In 1988 the college acquired the Squire Law Library building, designed by Charles Robert Cockerell, for its own library (see page 4.36), and later appointed John Simpson, an architect with a reputation for working in historical styles, to refit Salvin's library and the parts of the west range affected by this move. Simpson suggested that a version of Soane's scheme for the old hall be recreated, although thanks to Salvin's introduction of intermediate floors, the proportions are not as Soane intended. In the new Fellows' Dining Room Simpson relied on Cockerell's inspiration to create his own version of a richly decorated classical Greek interior.

ADDRESS Trinity Street
ACCESS none; visible from Trinity Lane

Anthony Salvin 1853–54, John Simpson 1997

Gonville and Caius College, Hall

Colleges to the north of King's College Chapel

Anthony Salvin 1853–54, John Simpson 1997

Gonville and Caius College, Tree Court

Alfred Waterhouse was a prolific and successful High Victorian architect who produced competent but overscaled buildings in both Oxford and Cambridge in the 1860s and 1870s. At Cambridge he also worked for Jesus, Pembroke (see page 5.58) and Girton (see page 4.30) Colleges besides Gonville and Caius, and at Oxford his building for Balliol College is almost as overbearing as Tree Court, though smaller.

Tree Court, so named after a planting scheme of c.1685, was rebuilt by Waterhouse in 1868–70 in an entirely inappropriate French Renaissance style, to increase substantially the college's accommodation. This included the reconstruction of the west range of Gonville Court (see page 4.34), where Waterhouse retained James Burrough's eighteenth-century elevation, and the construction of a new apse to the chapel. At the same time Waterhouse moved John Caius's Gate of Humility (see page 4.32) to the Master's Garden, inscribing, with unintended irony, his own new gate tower with the word 'Humilitatis'.

The new building, in two different coloured stones, has three tall storeys with an ornate attic and steep roofs, and its bulk dominates Trinity Street. Along Trinity Lane the scale is reduced in response to Gonville Court. The scheme's *pièce de résistance*, however, is the Disney-like fairyland tower that Waterhouse drew up as a stop to King's Parade. Displaying the worst architectural manners, this rudely challenges the calm classicism of James Gibbs's Senate House (see page 3.4) and memorably upstages the tower of Great St Mary's church (see page 2.14).

ADDRESS Trinity Street
ACCESS college open daily, 9.00–14.00; closed May and June

Alfred Waterhouse 1868–70

Colleges to the north of King's College Chapel

Alfred Waterhouse 1868–70

Gonville and Caius College, St Michael's Court

St Michael's Court, across Trinity Street from Gonville and Caius's main entrance, is named after the medieval church around which it is built. The northern part of the court is a redevelopment of property acquired by the college in 1887 along the south side of Rose Crescent, an attractive street of houses with shops below dating from c.1826. Aston Webb's design of 1901–03 is in the Tudor style, with an Arts and Crafts influence particularly noticeable at the entrance to Rose Crescent from Trinity Street. Recently the ground floor to Rose Crescent was converted by the college to small shops, and neatly detailed glass bay windows added.

Murray Easton's 1934–36 southern part of St Michael's Court was built on the site of houses similarly acquired by the college, and is a mixed-use development with shops on the ground floor facing Market Hill and Rose Crescent. Within the court the five-storey building is of warm Ketton stone with conservative timber sash windows. The rooms are accessed from a terrace raised above the shops.

On the Market Hill side, however, Easton felt free to work in the increasingly popular English Modern Movement style. This had been given impetus by Frederick Etchell who translated Le Corbusier's *Vers une architecture* (1923) as *Towards a Modern Architecture*, and in 1934 by F R S Yorke's *The Modern House*. Easton's response was to overlay the building with a projecting bay of white Portland stone above an open arcade. Crittall metal windows and string courses ending in a curve at the west end are used to give horizontal emphasis, while the bay stops short of Rose Crescent to mark its entrance.

ADDRESS Trinity Street, Market Hill
ACCESS college open daily, 9.00–14.00; closed May and June

Aston Webb 1901–03, Murray Easton 1934–36

Gonville and Caius College, St Michael's Court

Aston Webb 1901–03, Murray Easton 1934–36

Jesus College, Chapel and Cloister Court

The Benedictine nunnery of St Radegund, west of medieval Cambridge, was founded in 1133–38 and appropriated by John Alcock, Bishop of Ely, for the foundation of Jesus College in 1496. Alcock retained and adapted the buildings around the cloister, refacing them with brickwork and fitting Perpendicular Gothic windows and shallow-pitched roofs. He also converted the east range, previously the dormitory and chapter-house, into three floors of accommodation. The library was placed in the remodelled west range. In the north range the first-floor refectory was converted into the college's hall by the addition of a fine chestnut roof and a tall bay window. The cloister piers and arches were rebuilt in 1762–65 to designs by James Essex.

The conventual church, now the chapel, has twelfth-century Norman blocked windows in the north transept, and the crossing arches are late thirteenth-century Gothic. Alcock remodelled it by removing the aisles, extending the cloister into the north aisle, reroofing it and adding a bell-stage to the tower. He also converted the western part of the nave into three storeys of accommodation and lodgings for the Master.

In 1846–58 Augustus W N Pugin restored the early thirteenth-century chancel, replacing Alcock's shallow roof, and the east window with three lancet windows to match the others. He also designed the screen and other woodwork, incorporating earlier fragments, and the chancel glass. In 1865–69 George Bodley had William Morris decorate his new nave and tower ceilings, and in 1873–77 Edward Burne-Jones, Ford Madox Brown and William Morris reglazed the transept and nave windows.

ADDRESS Jesus Lane
ACCESS college open daily, 6.00–24.00; closed May and June

Twelfth–sixteenth and nineteenth centuries

Jesus College, Chapel and Cloister Court

Twelfth–sixteenth and nineteenth centuries

Jesus College, Outer Court

Jesus College is entered from Jesus Lane through two gate piers built by Robert Grumbold in 1703, with gates of c.1725. A pathway leads between high walls, that on the right dating partly from 1681, to the Master's Garden, and that on the left to the Fellows' Garden dating from 1608–09. At the end is the three-storey brick gate tower erected in 1500–03 when John Alcock, Bishop of Ely, was converting the nunnery of St Radegund into his new college (see page 4.44). The tower, with its original oak linenfold gates, has a four-centred arch with a crocketed ogee label supporting a niche. This contains a nineteenth-century statue of Alcock.

The range in which the gate tower stands was originally of two storeys, the eastern part being converted by Alcock from the nunnery guest house into the Master's Lodge. The bay window and porch date from 1886. The westerly part was built in 1503–07 as a grammar school and appropriated by the college in 1570. The third storey was added in 1718–20, and sash windows in 1791, but these, and the tower windows, were converted back to the original four-centred windows in 1880.

The gate tower leads to Outer Court, open to the west, which was given its present form in 1638–43 by the construction of the three-storey range opposite the gate tower. This was modelled on the east range, which was extended to meet it. This is one of the ranges around the original cloister, which was faced in brick and remodelled by Alcock after 1496 to provide three floors of accommodation. It contains Alcock's original library on the top floor, refitted in 1663–79, and his original Perpendicular Gothic archway to Cloister Court, now resited to the centre from the south end of the range.

ADDRESS Jesus Lane
ACCESS college open daily, 6.00–24.00; closed May and June

Early sixteenth and mid-seventeenth centuries

Early sixteenth and mid-seventeenth centuries

Jesus College, North Court

David Roberts ran a small but busy practice in Cambridge from 1946 to the 1980s, while also lecturing on Italian Renaissance architecture at the School of Architecture. One of the practice's strengths was residential buildings for the colleges, and examples of its work can be seen at Benson Court, Magdalene College, where Roberts was a Fellow, and at Trinity Hall, among others. Unlike other contemporary work in Cambridge, for example by Martin and Wilson, Arup Associates, Powell and Moya, and James Stirling, Roberts's designs are often low-key and undogmatic.

North Court was built to house 70 undergraduates, three graduates and two Fellows. It overlooks playing fields next to Alfred Waterhouse's 1870 red brick range, with which its yellow brick and angular forms are a total contrast. The L-shaped range is of three storeys, rising to four at the southern end, and appears to float above a semi-basement of changing rooms and ancillary spaces.

Roberts's ingenious plan is made up of a diagonal echelon of square spaces. The core of the building consists of squares set on the diagonal, alternately containing washrooms and octagonal stairs of in-situ concrete. Flanking the core are the rooms, each expressed by a diagonally projecting bay window. The spaces between are filled with recessed balconies whose brick balustrades, running parallel with the building, impart a feeling of horizontality. At roof level the diagonal walls of the rooms are extended up, resulting in a serrated skyline that reflects the building's plan.

ADDRESS Jesus Lane
ACCESS college open daily, 6.00–24.00; closed May and June

David Roberts 1963–66

Colleges to the north of King's College Chapel

David Roberts 1963–66

Jesus College, Quincentenary Library

In 1991 Evans and Shalev, best known for their Tate Gallery at St Ives, Cornwall, won the competition for a new court between the 1920s neo-Tudor block by Morley Horder and Jesus Lane. The Quincentenary Library is the only built part of the court to date and will eventually form the west range.

The library takes the form of a rectangular block with a small pavilion-like garden room appended to the west side. From the exterior the building appears severe and forbidding. The architectural language of buff stock brick, stone dressings to the openings and heavy Georgian-type windows seems a curious choice of style in the setting. The main entrance, from the east, is currently approached via Chapel Court and its location will seem a little incongruous until the new court is built to face it.

The interior consists of a vast barrel-vaulted space flanked by galleries and widens as it rises. The galleries contain book-lined alcoves and study carrels overlooking the void. The space is reminiscent of the vaulted libraries at Gonville and Caius, Newnham and New Hall (see pages 4.36, 5.48 and 4.58); however, unlike the earlier libraries where timber predominates, everything here is an ethereal white. The ground floor houses the entrance, cellular rooms and a broad staircase running up the central axis of the building. The architectural language of the interior differs from and is more successful than the exterior, and many of the details, such as the balconies with their square motifs, continue the language of Evans and Shalev's earlier buildings.

ADDRESS Jesus Lane
ACCESS college open daily, 6.00–24.00; closed May and June

Evans and Shalev 1996

Colleges to the north of King's College Chapel

Evans and Shalev 1996

Magdalene College, First Court

Benedictine monks studying at the university lived in a hostel on this site from 1428, and in 1483 the arrangement was formalised under the name Buckingham College. The north range including the chapel was built about this time, and the hall probably in 1519. Various Benedictine monasteries built houses beside each other to form the south side of the site, and by 1539 when the monastery at Croyland and the college were both dissolved First Court was complete with the exception of part of the west range by the gate. This was completed after the college was refounded in 1542 by Henry VIII's Lord Chancellor, Lord Audley of Warden, and retains its original gateway and gates of c.1585.

In 1733–56 the chapel was given a classical interior, but this and the rooms that had been added above were removed by John Buckler when he restored it in 1847–51. Buckler recreated the chapel's late medieval appearance and uncovered the original timber roof. In 1712 a Combination Room was created by inserting a floor above the kitchens to the south of the hall, and in 1714 the hall was fitted out in a classical style, and rooms created above it. The Prior's (later the Master's) Lodge was originally in the north-west corner of the court. In 1835 Buckler built a new lodge by Chesterton Lane, but this was demolished in the 1960s when the present lodge was built to designs by David Roberts.

The style of the buildings is largely late Tudor. In 1759–60 the external walls were stuccoed, and battlements were added in 1812–15. From 1955 the stucco was removed to reveal the original brick facing, the battlements replaced by plain eaves, and the slate roof retiled, returning the college to its early sixteenth-century appearance.

ADDRESS Magdalene Street
ACCESS college open daily, 9.00–18.30; closed mid-April to mid-June

Fifteenth–sixteenth centuries

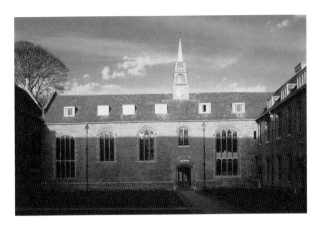

Fifteenth–sixteenth centuries

Magdalene College, Pepys Building

The Pepys Building is something of a mystery, since neither its date nor its architect is known. The building stands a short distance east of the original college and was projected as early as 1640, but construction probably started only in 1668–79. A central block connects two gabled wings, with staircases in the angles at the rear. The elevation away from the college appears quietly domestic. It has two storeys and attics and is of brick with stone dressings.

In 1677 Robert Hooke, scientist, astronomer and colleague of Christopher Wren, was paid for a design by the college, and two years later Samuel Pepys made the college a building loan. It is possible that the loan was used to build the present front elevation using Hooke's design. Certainly the three-storey colonnaded stone façade, completed before 1688, is architecturally distinguished, with its use of pediments over the windows, Ionic pilasters, and crowning balustrade. However, its handling of the classical language calls into question Hooke's authorship, at least of the details. The receding chimneys and expressed gable ends have led to the suggestion that the plan of the original building was H-shaped, with this elevation infilling the projecting wings.

Possibly the first-floor room, raised on a colonnade, was intended for a library even at this stage. Pepys' library was bequeathed to the college in 1703, the year of his death, and housed in the room over the colonnade in 1724. This was when the inscription, busts and decorative carving were added to the building, and when it acquired its present name.

ADDRESS Magdalene Street
ACCESS college open daily, 9.00–18.30; closed mid-April to mid-June

Mid- to late-seventeenth century

Magdalene College, Pepys Building

Mid- to late-seventeenth century

Magdalene College, Benson Court

To celebrate the fifth centenary in 1928 of the college's original foundation, Magdalene commissioned Edwin Lutyens to design a new court between Magdalene Street and Binn Brook, opposite the college's main entrance. Lutyens proposed demolishing the buildings along Magdalene Street to create space for a narrow three-sided court parallel with the road and open to the river. Only the west range was completed, and the sixteenth-century houses on Magdalene Street survive.

Benson Court was designed during the later classical period of Lutyens's career, but his use here of narrow hand-made red bricks and stone mullioned windows refers to the late Tudor origins of the college. A continuous plinth, band and cornice of Weldon stone unify the composition. The roof has a double ridge between which tall chimneys rise, giving the impression from both sides that they are on the far side of the roof, and allowing Lutyens to devise an interesting elevational treatment of two gables and a chimney facing the river.

Five stairs rise from the court. The stone doorcases and swagged coats of arms above imply the existence of five houses, a further reference to the south range of First Court (see page 4.52). By framing the doorways in a triangle of windows and devising special dormers above, Lutyens creates a subtle rhythm between the gable ends of the building. Inside, the oak staircases were, according to Lutyens, designed with individually carved newel posts to help undergraduates recognise their own staircases at night.

Sadly this is Lutyens's only building in Cambridge, though a design of his was used for Silver Street Bridge.

ADDRESS Magdalene Street
ACCESS college open daily, 9.00–18.30; closed mid-April to mid-June

Edwin Lutyens 1930–32

Edwin Lutyens 1930–32

New Hall

New Hall, which was the third Cambridge women's college to be founded, occupied an early nineteenth-century house in Silver Street from 1954 to 1964 until a grant from the Wolfsen Foundation funded the building of a new college.

The first phase, 1962–64, consisted of a sunken landscaped court at the eastern end of the site, with an entrance off Buckingham Road; the cylindrical entrance and forecourt are recent additions (see page 4.60). On the eastern side of the court is the exotic domed first-floor dining hall, cruciform in plan with a central servery rising theatrically through the floor from the kitchens below. Projecting forward from the hall is the galleried Junior Combination Room. The west range contains the library, which, following Cambridge precedent, is a long full-height tunnel-vaulted nave with niches and galleries containing the book stacks and reading spaces. The north and south ranges contain offices and a pleasant broad glazed cloister, that to the north providing an axial route through the college.

The second phase, 1964–66, added a residential court to the north. The master-planning successfully alludes to the collegiate court tradition, yet forms a spatially more open type in response to the landscaped setting. The atmosphere is calm, light and airy. The architectural language makes obvious references to Louis Kahn's work in the formal discipline of the plan, the use of platonic forms, and heavy brickwork walls and piers. Yet somehow the use of pure white brickwork and concrete, and the imagery of a domed roof seem misplaced for a women's college.

ADDRESS Huntingdon Road
ACCESS apply at porter's lodge

Chamberlin Powell and Bon 1962–66

Chamberlin Powell and Bon 1962–66

New Hall, Kaetsu Educational and Cultural Centre

Chamberlin Powell and Bon's buildings for New Hall (see page 4.58) were given statutory listing in 1990. However, phase three of the master-plan remained unbuilt. In 1994 funding became available from a Japanese college to add further accommodation to the college. Frank Woods of Austin-Smith:Lord, previously of Chamberlin Powell and Bon, was given the sensitive commission. The new buildings continue the earlier pattern of platonic forms containing the communal rooms, set against plain residential ranges. However, their architecture alludes more to the late modernists, such as Richard Meier, rather than the early modernism of Louis Kahn and Le Corbusier.

The new work provides a much-needed formal entrance from a new forecourt off Buckingham Road, centred around a low rotunda containing the porters' lodge. At the west end of the college's axial cloister are two new ranges of residential accommodation that run north–south into the garden, and a further range which forms a new sunken parking courtyard. This range contains residential accommodation in the body of the building and, in a distinctive rotunda at the end nearest Huntingdon Road, a design education centre for the Kaetsu Educational Foundation, containing a lecture theatre, seminar rooms and a top-floor dining room. While the residential ranges are a polite reinterpretation of the original buildings, the design of the Kaetsu Centre, a five-storey limestone drum pierced by the glazed corners of an elongated cube, is a more assertive and refined essay in late modernism.

ADDRESS Huntingdon Road
ACCESS apply at porter's lodge

Austin-Smith:Lord 1994–96

Austin-Smith:Lord 1994–96

Queens' College, Boathouse

The commission for the design of a new college boathouse plus adjacent speculative housing was awarded following an architect/developer competition.

The boathouse design follows the traditional typology: ground-floor storage for the college 'eights' (eight-man boats) and communal facilities above. From the river the building reads as three glazed gabled pavilions raised on a single-storey brick base. The central pavilion contains a coaching room and changing rooms, and the outer pavilions each house three flats for graduates – an unusual inclusion for a boathouse. The adjacent terrace houses have narrow frontages that develop the gable theme of the boathouse. Here each three-storey house has half a gable. The stepping plan expresses the cross-wall construction and provides an enjoyable syncopated rhythm, the glazed river elevation with its first-floor balconies contrasting with the solid rear walls on the entry side.

Both buildings demonstrate the familiar modest aesthetic developed by the architects in their former incarnation as Cambridge Design Architects, a kind of extended vernacular consisting of familiar typological forms in local materials – here Stamford Grey bricks, timber and clay roof tiles. The language of the details fragments the elements giving the building small-scale interest. The eaves detail with its expressed rafters and concealed gutters is a particular delight. The emphasis on the simplicity of the forms and on 'making', places the building firmly and successfully within an Arts and Crafts lineage.

ADDRESS on the Cam, adjacent to Victoria Bridge
ACCESS none; visible from river walk and Victoria Bridge

Design Group Cambridge 1990

Queens' College, Boathouse

Design Group Cambridge 1990

St John's College, First Court

Lady Margaret Beaufort, mother of Henry VIII, founded St John's College in 1511, and Bishop Fisher directed the building of the college on the site of the suppressed Hospital of St John the Evangelist during the early sixteenth century. The thirteenth-century hospital infirmary and chapel were integrated into the north range of a new court, First Court, until they were demolished to make way for George Gilbert Scott's chapel in 1863 (see page 4.72). The master mason for the new buildings was William Swayne, who also worked at Trinity, King's and Christ's Colleges.

The St John's Street elevation has a quintessentially medieval flavour with its gatehouse, tall chimneys and gables. The three-storey brick gate-house with angled turrets has a Tudor linenfold panelled door above which is a fine display of painted heraldic carving. The figure of St John in the niche is by George Woodroffe (1662). Inside the court the two-storey west and east ranges, of brick decorated with a diaper pattern of vitrified headers, have a battlemented parapet and irregularly placed hooded windows of two and three lights. The refacing of the south range in ashlar by James Essex in 1772–75, together with the replacement of the north range with Scott's chapel, means that the court no longer has the stylistic unity it once possessed. The hall, which lies north of the screens passage in the west range, is sixteenth century except for the last bay, which was added in 1862 when the chapel was constructed. It retains its original impressive hammerbeam roof and some original panelling, though the decorative scheme dates from 1868.

ADDRESS St John's Street
ACCESS college open Monday to Friday, 10.00–17.30; Saturday and Sunday, 9.30–17.30; admission charge March to October

William Swayne (master mason) 1511–20

Colleges to the north of King's College Chapel

William Swayne (master mason) 1511–20

St John's College, Second Court

The Countess of Shrewsbury gave the funds for the building of Second Court, which leads directly on from First Court (see page 4.64). The college required the new buildings to follow the style of First Court and the result is that the new ranges are almost indistinguishable from the east range, built some 80 years earlier. The masons of Second Court added the Jacobean-flavoured top gables to the older range, and the angle turret at the south end.

The new ranges are of three storeys with a repeated fenestration pattern of three-light windows with hooded mouldings. The top storey is treated like an attic and each window has a gable above. The doorways to the staircases have four-centred arches, again following those in First Court. The rather dull consistency of the façades is broken on the north and south ranges by a central first-floor oriel window, with Jacobean strapwork decoration on the sill and open strapwork cresting on top, and more significantly by the Shrewsbury Tower in the centre of the west range. The design of the tower with its four angled turrets and battlements is clearly modelled on the gateway to First Court. Here, the centrepiece is a statue of the Countess of Shrewsbury by Thomas Burman (1671).

Internally, the south and west ranges contain chambers, while the first floor of the north range originally housed the long Master's Gallery. It was later shortened at both ends to include staircases and its use changed to the Senior Combination Room. The plaster ceiling of 1600–01, divided by decorated bands into tessellated lozenge shapes, is particularly fine.

ADDRESS St John's Street
ACCESS college open Monday to Friday, 10.00–17.30; Saturday and Sunday, 9.30–17.30; admission charge March to October

Ralph Symons and Gilbert Wigge (masons) 1598–1602

Ralph Symons and Gilbert Wigge (masons) 1598–1602

St John's College, Third Court and Library

The first building to follow the completion of Second Court (see page 4.66) was the library, built in 1623–25, which continued the axis of the court's north range. The benefactor for the new library was Bishop William of Lincoln; the designer was probably Henry Man, carpenter.

The plan of the new library followed the accepted typology by housing the books in a single volume on the upper floor and using the ground floor for other purposes, in this case as chambers. The elevation to Third Court, later foreshortened by the addition of the west range, has a plain Tudor brickwork façade of eight bays with stone string courses and dressings to the openings, and distinctive battlements with pointed-arch tops on rectangular bases. The tall two-light windows to the library have two-centred heads and tracery making them the earliest example of Gothic Revival in Cambridge. The library is entered on the first floor through a heavy Jacobean-style entrance at the east end. The interior is notable for its bookcases attached to the walls and linked at cornice level, the panelled roof, and the large bay window, of mixed Tudor and Gothic design, overlooking the river at the west end.

In 1669 further ranges containing three storeys of chambers were built to form the closed Third Court. The materials and battlements of the library are continued. However, the overall design is more elaborate and distinctly seventeenth century. The south range has a classical ground-floor stone cloister, first-floor cross-type windows like those used at Christ's College in 1640, and a central almost baroque frontispiece.

ADDRESS St John's Street
ACCESS college open Monday to Friday, 10.00–17.30; Saturday and Sunday, 9.30–17.30; admission charge March to October

Henry Man (carpenter) 1623–25, 1669–73

Henry Man (carpenter) 1623–25, 1669–73

St John's College, New Court and Bridge of Sighs

New Court was the first new building at St John's College since the completion of Third Court (see page 4.68) 150 years earlier. The commission for additional student sets responded to the great increase in student numbers in the early nineteenth century. Its architect, Thomas Rickman, was an acknowledged expert on English Gothic architecture, on which he published the first systematic treatise in 1817. New Court is Rickman's only building in Cambridge, and probably his most ambitious secular building.

New Court extended the college's memorable sequence of courts by adding a fourth court on an open site on the far side of the River Cam. It was linked back to Third Court by a memorable covered Gothic bridge, known as the Bridge of Sighs, designed by Rickman's partner, Henry Hutchinson. Despite the romantic imagery, Third Court has an extremely formal, almost classical, plan consisting of a symmetrical court with three sides of residential ranges, and a screen closing the fourth, south side. The court has a central axis formed by a gateway in the screen and an elaborate tower in the centre of the north range. The two identical pavilion-like east and west ranges further emphasise the symmetry. If the composition is rather predictable, the detail is a pure Tudor-Gothic delight. Pinnacles, embattled parapets, oriel and arch-headed windows, polygonal angle turrets and a spectacular lantern with thin flying buttresses and pinnacles combine to produce a romantic silhouette.

ADDRESS St John's Street
ACCESS college open Monday to Friday, 10.00–17.30; Saturday and Sunday, 9.30–17.30; admission charge March to October

Thomas Rickman and Henry Hutchinson 1827–31

Thomas Rickman and Henry Hutchinson 1827–31

St John's College, Chapel

In 1863 St John's College decided to build a new chapel and to enlarge the hall. This meant destroying the thirteenth-century chapel and north range of First Court (see page 4.64). The position of the old chapel is inscribed into the lawn. The architect for the new chapel was George Gilbert Scott who in 1858 had completed a Gothic chapel for Exeter College, Oxford.

By placing his chapel further to the north, Scott enlarged the court, opening it up to St John's Street. The layout of the chapel repeated the Oxford model in which the antechapel is placed in a transverse position at the west end of the chapel. Thus, the antechapel and its entrance lie in the north-east corner of First Court and are marked by the huge square-topped tower over the crossing. The cathedral-like chancel is long and tall, with a polygonal apse at the east end. This is disengaged from the rest of the college buildings, making the chapel appear huge and curiously out of place when seen from St John's Street.

Scott justified his choice of late thirteenth-century English Gothic by its coincidence with the date of the original college chapel. The construction is of Ancaster stone and the details, from the pointed traceried windows in the chapel to the pinnacles on the tower, have an almost mechanical accuracy. The splendid single volume of the chancel and choir has a fine rib-vaulted roof that springs from marble columns and carved niches housing saints. The thirteenth-century piscina behind the altar was taken from the old chapel.

ADDRESS St John's Street
ACCESS college open Monday to Friday, 10.00–17.30; Saturday and Sunday, 9.30–17.30; admission charge March to October

George Gilbert Scott 1863–69

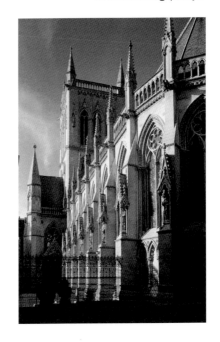

George Gilbert Scott 1863–69

St John's College, Cripps Building

Following Alvar Aalto's rejection of this commission for 200 undergraduate rooms and Fellows' sets, both Denys Lasdun and Powell and Moya were asked to submit proposals. Powell and Moya's scheme was selected.

The scheme is accessed primarily through New Court. It takes the form of a four-storey linear block that cranks to form a number of new courts, informal spaces and events. The head of the block addresses the River Cam then returns to form a three-sided courtyard against the back of New Court. Unfortunately, the single-storey west range was demolished in 1987 and replaced by the unsympathetic Fisher Building. The block continues by hopping over Bin Brook, alluding to an inhabited bridge, forming a second court with the twelfth-century Pythagoras Building.

The accommodation spans between heroically scaled Portland stone-clad piers and is lifted to create a continuous cloister at ground level allowing the landscape to flow beneath the building. The cloister gives access to open staircases off which groups of student study-bedrooms are located. The external articulation is strong and simple and composed of alternating flat-faced and projecting bays. These bays are broken down into a finer scale by the expressed concrete floor slabs, delicate transoms and mullions, and infill panels of glass or lead. The rooftop houses Fellows' flats, roof terraces and expressed lead-clad water tanks give a modulated skyline. The subtlety of this scheme is undeniable: it is at once picturesque and formal, traditional and modern.

ADDRESS St John's Street
ACCESS college open Monday to Friday, 10.00–17.30; Saturday and Sunday, 9.30–17.30; admission charge March to October

Powell and Moya 1963–67

Colleges to the north of King's College Chapel

Powell and Moya 1963–67

St John's College, Library

In 1985 St John's College finally addressed the problem of cramped library accommodation by launching a competition for a new library. Edward Cullinan Architects won the competition with an ingenious solution that retained and replanned the nineteenth-century Penrose Building, connected it to the adjacent seventeenth-century Upper Library, and added new accommodation in the form of transepts.

The transepts make certain material and linguistic references to the Penrose Building, for example by repeating the gable and using the same brick and stone string courses. This suggests a quiet contextual approach. However, the attempts at mannerism, for instance in the paired columns joined at the bottom, and the corners of glass set behind stone columns, make the building feel overworked. Additionally, the detail of the lantern over the crossing is a linguistic oddity even if its functional remit, a vent as part of a passive environmental control system, is commendable.

Internally the building is more successful. The spatial planning works effortlessly to provide a great variety of spaces, allowing the library to be used in different ways. The ground-floor lecture rooms of the Penrose Building have been turned into a double-height entrance hall entered from the new portico in Chapel Court, while the upper floors house the bookstacks and the reroofed attic level is used as a computer room. The upper floors of the transepts provide particularly nicely crafted study spaces with fine views.

ADDRESS St John's Street
ACCESS college open Monday to Friday, 10.00–17.30; Saturday and Sunday, 9.30–17.30; admission charge March to October

Edward Cullinan Architects 1994

Edward Cullinan Architects 1994

Sidney Sussex College, Hall Court

Hall Court was built on the site of an earlier Franciscan friary soon after Sidney Sussex College's foundation in 1594. The three-sided court was entered from the street through a central gateway set in a wall. The range opposite contained the hall at the north end, and at the south end the Master's Lodge above the kitchens. The red-brick building was of two storeys with substantial dormers. A central tower led to the hall, and there was a tower at each corner.

In 1749–52 the hall was refitted internally in the classical style by James Burrough, who also installed a plaster ceiling under the original hammer-beam roof, while retaining the original bay window. Burrough also redesigned the entrance gateway.

Jeffry Wyatville remodelled the entire college in 1821–33, while retaining the earlier hall. Borrough's gateway was resited in Jesus Lane, and a new entrance made under a tower at the street end of the south range of Hall Court. This cleverly united Hall Court with the later Chapel Court to the south (see page 4.80) to give the college an E-shaped plan. Wyatville projected the hall range into the court between the two original side towers, which now appear as recessed corners, and designed massive buttresses on the garden side. He also extended the walls to a third storey in front of the original dormers, and added small dormers above. To make the buildings conform to his idea of Tudor-Gothic, Wyatville added battlemented parapets and crow-stepped gables everywhere, and covered the walls with a cement facing. For the new entrance tower, and the walls in front of the hall and chapel, he used stone.

ADDRESS Sidney Street
ACCESS college open daily, 9.00–17.00; closed May and June

Ralph Symons 1596–98, remodelled by Jeffry Wyatville 1821–33

Colleges to the north of King's College Chapel

Ralph Symons 1596–98, remodelled by Jeffry Wyatville 1821–33

Sidney Sussex College, Chapel Court

In 1602, just four years after the completion of Hall Court (see page 4.78), a building to its south remaining from the Franciscan Friary was adapted to provide a chapel on the ground floor with a library above. The south range followed in c.1628.

The chapel and library were subsequently rebuilt and lengthened in 1776–82 to a plain classical design by James Essex, and both chapel and south ranges remodelled to designs by Jeffry Wyatville in 1832–33 as part of his scheme for remodelling the entire college (see page 4.78). His original proposals for using windows in Early English Gothic in this court were abandoned in favour of the Tudor-Gothic he used in Hall Court. Wyatville retained the 1778 library fittings and added a bell turret to the main elevation.

The chapel was more than doubled in length and entirely remodelled internally to designs by T H Lyon in 1910–12 and 1920–25. His low white plaster barrel vault, full-height oak panelling and stalls that freely adapt Christopher Wren's details, and marble floor (with steps marking the length of Essex's chapel) make this, in Nikolaus Pevsner's words, 'a remarkably fine piece of ecclesiastical architecture'. Lyon also designed the neo-Georgian range to the side of the chapel by the Master's Garden.

To the south of the chapel lies Sussex Street, an interesting piece of pre-war urban design in the neo-Georgian style for the college by E R Barrow. The south side of 1928–32, a shallow crescent, has houses with houses above, while the straight north side of 1938–39 has shops with student rooms above accessed from a raised terrace on the college side.

ADDRESS Sidney Street
ACCESS college open daily, 9.00–17.00; closed May and June

Early seventeenth century, remodelled by Jeffry Wyatville 1832–33

Early seventeenth century, remodelled by Jeffry Wyatville 1832–33

Trinity College, Great Court

When in 1546 Henry VIII founded Trinity, Cambridge's largest college, the site of the present Great Court was crossed by a public thoroughfare and occupied by three colleges and six hostels, one of which is mentioned by the reeve in Geoffrey Chaucer's *The Canterbury Tales*. The thoroughfare was closed, and the main court of King's Hall, founded by Edward III in 1337, retained as the nucleus of the new college. The Great Gate and the range to each side had been started in 1490 to provide a new entrance to King's Hall from the High Street, and the upper stages of the tower were completed in 1528–35. On the south side Michael House and the hostels adjoining Trinity Lane were adapted to form a second court. Work on the college included construction of a chapel (see page 4.84).

Under the Mastership of Thomas Nevile (1593–1615) a more ambitious scheme to form one great court was pursued. In 1598–1602 the east range was extended southwards, the south range (including Queen's Gate) rebuilt, and various parts of the former King's Hall protruding into Great Court were cleared away. King Edward's Tower, built in 1328–32 as the original entrance to King's Hall, was rebuilt adjacent to the chapel from its original position. The northern part of the west range was rebuilt to accommodate the Master's Lodge, and to its east a new library completed the north range. The fountain was built at the same time, though rebuilt in 1715–16, and in 1604–05 the new hall, with its hammer-beam roof and strapwork screen, was built to designs by Ralph Symons. The original hall alongside was replaced in 1771–74 with a classical building designed by James Essex.

ADDRESS Trinity Street
ACCESS college open daily, 10.00–17.30; closed May and June; admission charge March to November

Late fifteenth–eighteenth centuries

Late fifteenth–eighteenth centuries

Trinity College, Chapel

Trinity College chapel was built on the site of the chapel of King's Hall (see page 4.82). Although the college was founded by Henry VIII, the chapel was erected largely during the reign of Mary I. It is entirely of Perpendicular Gothic, lacking any Renaissance details that Henry might have introduced.

The chapel is a simple rectangle of 12 bays with tall relatively plain windows divided by buttresses. The timber roof is shallow and divided into panels. The large west window was blocked up when King Edward's Tower was rebuilt between the chapel and the old library in 1599 as part of the works to form Great Court (see page 4.82).

The east window was also blocked up in the early eighteenth century when the internal fittings were renewed. The classical timber screen, which divides the space into antechapel and chapel, the organ case, choir panelling, stalls and fine reredos, are all of the early eighteenth century, in the style of Christopher Wren, although the designer's name is not known. The marble floor is also of this period.

The antechapel serves as a hall of fame for the college, with white marble statues and busts of the great. Many are Victorian, but Sir Isaac Newton, by Louis Roubilliac, is of 1775, and that of Alfred Tennyson is of 1909. The panelling is nineteenth century. The south porch was added in 1868–73 to designs by Arthur Blomfield, who also refaced the previously rendered south and east elevations in stone, and added new glass to the windows.

ADDRESS Trinity Street
ACCESS college open daily, 10.00–17.30; closed May and June; admission charge March to November

Colleges to the north of King's College Chapel

1555–67

Trinity College, Nevile's Court

Nevile's Court was given to Trinity College by Thomas Nevile, under whose Mastership Great Court (see page 4.82) had been completed a few years earlier.

When first built it was three-fifths its present length, and its west side was closed to the river by a wall with a central arched gateway surmounted by an ornate Jacobean superstructure. Nevile's Gate now stands in Trinity Lane, outside Bishop's Hostel. The court was extended in the same style to its present length in 1676–85, in conjunction with the construction of Christopher Wren's library (see page 4.90), both to provide further accommodation and to improve its proportions. In 1682–85 the tribunal and raised terrace at the east end, probably designed by Wren, were built by Robert Grumbold to provide an axial response to the library, then nearing completion.

When built, the classical ground-floor arcaded cloister, redolent of Renaissance Italy, was enjoying a fashion in England. Above it, between each window, were short columns supported on lion-head corbels with superimposed columns dividing the major bays, all used as rainwater pipes. The top-floor windows were treated as dormers with steeply pitched stone gables, and there were garrets in the roof above these. As now, the staircase towers and chimney stacks were on the sides away from the court.

James Essex's 1755–58 remodelling stripped the buildings of its Jacobean details, and renewed the roofs to provide balustraded parapets similar to the library's, in place of the dormers.

ADDRESS Trinity Street
ACCESS college open daily, 10.00–17.30; closed May and June; admission charge March to November

1605–12 and 1676–85, remodelled by James Essex 1755–58

1605–12 and 1676–85, remodelled by James Essex 1755–58

Trinity College, Bishop's Hostel

Bishop's Hostel was built to replace Garrett Hostel, with money given by John Hackett, Bishop of Lichfield and Coventry and a Fellow of the college. The builder was Robert Minchin, carpenter, of Bletchingdon, Oxfordshire, whose original contract is preserved in the college library. Minchin had worked for Christopher Wren at Trinity College, Oxford.

The building is of two storeys with attics, and has five sets of rooms on each floor. It is of brick with stone dressings, and there is a prominent cornice. The plan is U-shaped. The central bay between the two projecting wings is flanked by full-height Ionic pilasters supporting an entablature and a triangular pediment. This forms a grand entrance that leads to one of the sets of rooms, and not, as might be expected, to an entrance hall. There are instead two staircases, one in each wing, reached from the corner doorways.

Bishop's Hostel has a comfortable domestic quality typical of larger houses of Restoration England. The dormer windows were originally pedimented but were replaced in the eighteenth century, and the cross-shaped mullions and transoms of the main windows, replaced when Arthur Blomfield restored the building in 1877, were originally much stouter. The modern chimneys are similar to the originals.

ADDRESS Trinity Lane
ACCESS college open daily, 10.00–17.30; closed May and June; admission charge March to November

Robert Minchin (carpenter) 1670–71

Robert Minchin (carpenter) 1670–71

Trinity College, Library

Christopher Wren abandoned one idea for a domed circular library between the arms of Nevile's Court (see page 4.86) in favour of an elongated pavilion closing the end of the court, which was extended to meet it. The library is in Wren's mature classical style, based on Italian precedents. The east elevation has an arcade with three-quarter Roman Doric columns, superimposed by an Ionic order framing arched windows, and a balustraded parapet above. The more solid river elevation has a plainer though no less majestic treatment, with three grand portals.

The library is on the first floor above the flood plane, while the Nevile's Court cloister is continued as a double-width cloister below. The library floor is at the same level as the first floor of the court, and Wren achieved this by infilling the arches on the east elevation, an idea he had seen in Paris. This gave greater height in the library, allowing the projecting bookcases – concealing iron ties supporting the floor – to be placed below rather than between the windows, thus providing further space for wall cases. The entrance is through a square pavilion to the north, which Wren's design would have repeated to the south. Entrances at the end meant there was no reason for a central emphasis to the block, and this was limited to four statues on the east balustrade.

Inside, a central chequered marble aisle leads to freestanding reading desks in alcoves raised one step between the projecting oak bookcases. Wren also designed the desks and the bookcases. The limewood carving is by Grinling Gibbons; the plaster busts on the bookcases and other statues are mostly by leading sculptors of the mid-eighteenth century.

ADDRESS Trinity Street
ACCESS college open daily, 10.00–17.30; closed May and June; admission charge March to November; library open daily, 12.00–14.00

Christopher Wren 1676–90

Colleges to the north of King's College Chapel

Christopher Wren 1676–90

Trinity College, New Court

William Wilkins started New Court in the same year that he designed New Court at Corpus Christi College (see page 5.6), and just a year before he designed Front Court at King's College (see page 5.42). New Court predates Thomas Rickman's New Court at St John's College (see page 4.70) by four years. All are in the Gothic Revival style, although Wilkins at first produced a neo-classical design for Trinity College.

The court backs on to the south side of Nevile's Court (see page 4.86), and sits astride the route from Trinity Lane to James Essex's 1764–65 Trinity Bridge. Two offset gate towers mark this route. Like Wilkins's other Cambridge schemes of this time, the style is Tudor-Gothic. There are three storeys, with attics behind an embattled parapet. The north, south and east ranges are each symmetrical, though different, and all display a mixture of Gothic windows, oriels, niches, turrets and gables, tied together by string courses. The river façade is stone-clad and the other main elevations are cement rendered in a pinkish stone colour.

A cloistered walk on the north range behind Nevile's Court was demolished in 1868.

ADDRESS Trinity Street
ACCESS college open daily, 10.00–17.00; closed May and June; admission charge March to November

William Wilkins 1823–25

William Wilkins 1823–25

Trinity College, Blue Boar Court

Blue Boar Court is reached through Anthony Salvin's 1859–68 Whewell's Court opposite the college's main entrance on Trinity Street. It is an ingenious scheme tucked into the centre of the city block. The constraints on the architects were considerable: the existing perimeter buildings had to be retained and their servicing arrangements accommodated. Also to be kept was the college's rather unsuccessful 1968–72 ziggurat-like Wolfsen Building by Architects Co-Partnership.

The strategy adopted was to extend the first-floor podium on which the Wolfsen Building sat to cover the whole of the site and to create a series of linked first-floor courts, Blue Boar Court being the largest and most successful. The courts are formed by the new student accommodation, planned in traditional staircase groups, and various conference facilities. The geometry of the courts is relaxed and informal, simply taking on the incidental geometries of the site. The main entrance to the scheme is from Green Street but there are also minor entrances from surrounding streets through existing buildings.

The architects have a long track record of Oxford and Cambridge student housing and have developed typologies and an architectural language sensitive to the medieval town context. Blue Boar Court continues this vocabulary of fragmented forms, pitched roofs, stock brickwork, jettied bays, clerestories, towers and oriel windows, both suggesting accretion and also to reduce the scale. This is a masterly piece of infill providing students with well-designed study-bedrooms in an environment that refers to the Oxbridge tradition without being a slave to it.

ADDRESS Green Street
ACCESS none; partly visible from the street

MacCormac Jamieson Prichard and Wright 1990

Colleges to the north of King's College Chapel

MacCormac Jamieson Prichard and Wright 1990

Trinity College, Burrell's Field

This extremely successful housing resulted from a competition held in 1988. The brief was for 80 study-bedrooms, two Fellows' flats and ancillary accommodation on a large triangular landscaped site between Trinity Fellows' Garden and Grange Road, which contained some Edwardian houses, two 1970s student residences by David Roberts, and a now-demolished house by Patrick Hodgkinson.

MacCormac Jamieson Prichard rejected the Cambridge court typology in favour of a layout that alluded more to the formal planning of an early eighteenth-century landscape garden. In a grand formal statement a brick plinth was extended along the edge of the site running parallel with Bin Brook, thus raising the development above the flood plane. From the Fellows' Garden the plinth reads as a moated city wall on which one- and two-storey blocks and four-storey pavilions, or towers, alternate with verandahs. Various axes intersect a central promenade at 90 degrees: the bridge over the brook straddled by defensive towers, a formal garden in front of one of the existing houses, and a pool and new common room which integrate one of Roberts's buildings into the composition, together providing a sequence of delightful and varied vistas.

The 45-degree geometry inherent in the triangular site appears again in the design of the towers. They contain two study-bedrooms and a shared kitchen on each level. Each room has a triangular bay window placed centrally in the monolithic buff brick façade. Hence, the towers read as a brick cube intersected by a diagonal glass cube. This device, together with the floating roofs, shows a clear debt to the early work of the American architect Frank Lloyd Wright.

ADDRESS Grange Road
ACCESS none; visible from the street

MacCormac Jamieson Prichard 1995

MacCormac Jamieson Prichard 1995

Trinity Hall, Front Court

Trinity Hall, then known as The Hall of the Holy Trinity, was founded by William Bateman, Bishop of Norwich, in 1350 when building started. The chapel in the south range was complete by 1366, and the Master's Lodge, hall and kitchens in the west range before 1374. The north and east ranges contain chambers. The college was originally entered through South Court. In the late sixteenth century the library, forming part of a new open court, was added to the west. The early appearance of the buildings may be seen from North Court, but what is now seen within Front Court is the refacing in ashlar of the two-storey north, south and west ranges carried out by James Burrough in 1742–45. Burrough's refacing was in a restrained Palladian manner with repeated plain window surrounds, string courses and a plain parapet. Only the two large round-headed windows to the chapel break the pattern. The hall passage is given emphasis by a heavy pedimented door surround, the raising of the parapet into a pediment and a rooftop lantern. Odd baroque touches, such as the swags on the north range, are added for decoration. The chapel had been modernised internally by Andrews Jelfe, mason, in 1729–30 with a shallow plaster tunnel vault, and a simple organ gallery and reredos. Burrough's 1743–45 internal remodelling of the hall is more exuberant and has an almost rococo feel.

The three-storey east range, originally refaced and remodelled by Burrough to house a new college entrance from Trinity Lane, gained a third storey when it was rebuilt in a restrained Italianate style by Anthony Salvin after a fire in 1852.

ADDRESS Trinity Lane
ACCESS apply at porter's lodge

Mid-fourteenth century, refaced by James Burrough 1742–45

Mid-fourteenth century, refaced by James Burrough 1742–45

Trinity Hall, Boulton House

Space restrictions on their inner-city site led Trinity Hall to find a new development site on open land north-west of the city. Boulton House sits adjacent to Darwin College's Wychfield House between the Huntingdon Road and Storey's Way. The building houses 32 undergraduate study-bedrooms, two Fellows' flats, a common room, kitchen, laundry and other service rooms.

Despite its close proximity to two existing red-brick buildings, Boulton House is a four-storey, white, precast concrete-framed pavilion. The major façades consist of seven bays made up of a frame of expressed columns and spandrel panels infilled with large bay windows, one for each study-bedroom. The rooms face north and south and are accessed from a central corridor. They are raised above the ground floor, providing a covered colonnade beneath. The communal accommodation is on the ground floor and is detailed with black-framed glazing with planes of red brick alluding materially to the adjacent buildings. A charming smaller three-storey square pavilion to the south of Boulton House and designed in the same mode was a later addition, also by Arup Associates.

Boulton House was the fifth residential college building designed by Arup Associates in Oxford and Cambridge. All share a preoccupation with the idea of the pavilion type, the repeated precast concrete exoskeleton and the ground-floor cloister. Boulton House is arguably the best of their early work, though it does not match up to the refinement of the 1974–76 Sir Thomas White Building at St John's College, Oxford.

ADDRESS Huntingdon Road, next to Wychfield House
ACCESS none; visible from the approach road

Arup Associates 1967–68

Arup Associates 1967–68

King's College Chapel and colleges to its south

Clare Hall

Clare Hall was founded in 1966 as a college for graduates. Its architect, Ralph Erskine, British-born but since 1939 living and working in Sweden, was from 1956 a member of Team x. This group of architects and town planners investigated ways of reinvigorating modern architecture through the introduction of human, as opposed to purely aesthetic, values. Erskine's work, including his housing schemes at Byker in Newcastle, and at Newmarket and Milton Keynes, introduced new standards of communality, as does his building for Clare Hall. Of Clare Hall, Erskine wrote, 'we wished to achieve an open-ended and attractive environment which was free from memories of medieval and Renaissance monumentality or opulence, to ally ourselves with new society builders rather than the establishment'.

Two walkways, 'Family Walk' and 'Scholars' Walk', cut through the scheme from the college's raised entrances under the cantilevered wings of the President's Lodge. They step down to the south, as do the sloping aluminium-covered roofs, as a result of the ingenious section that places car parking in a semi-basement. These walks structure the site into a social and educational building to the east, four courtyard houses in the centre and a range of flats at the west, whose balconies overlook the shared garden. Bay windows, balconies and porches as well as the playful treatment of the rainwater chutes ensure that the walks encourage social interaction and never appear dull.

Until the advent of Robinson College (see page 5.84), this area was a leafy backwater of large houses to which Erskine's low forms and red brickwork, enlivened by typically 'Scandinavian' motifs, relate well.

ADDRESS Herschel Road
ACCESS external common areas generally accessible

Ralph Erskine 1968–69

Clare Hall

Ralph Erskine 1968–69

Corpus Christi College, Old Court

Corpus Christi Old Court is remarkable in largely preserving the form and appearance of the original mid-fourteenth-century college buildings. Building started in 1352, when the college was founded, and was complete by 1377. This was the first closed college courtyard to be built in Cambridge, and it gives a good idea of others that have subsequently been redeveloped or refaced.

The unpretentious entrance was originally through the gateway in the north range. The Master's Lodge was at the east end of the south range, and the hall in the centre. The hall is marked by a bay window, given its square form in the eighteenth century, and two four-centred Tudor windows. It now houses the servery. To its west is the tall new hall built in 1825–26 as part of William Wilkins's New Court (see page 5.6).

The two-storey court is built of random rubble stonework, with steeply pitched tiled roofs and simple overhanging eaves. The roofs were originally open internally, but were converted to garrets in the sixteenth century when the chimneys were built, though the present dormer windows are eighteenth century. Buttresses were added in the early sixteenth and seventeenth centuries to strengthen the walls. Many of the windows have been remodelled over the years, but some retain their original Gothic form.

Initially, St Bene't (see page 2.2) served as the college chapel. In 1544–53 two small chapels were added to the south side of the chancel and joined to the college by a two-storey brick gallery. In 1579 a new chapel was built south of Old Court and linked to it with another gallery, but these were demolished when New Court was built.

ADDRESS Trumpington Street
ACCESS college open daily, 14.00–16.00; closed May and June

1352–77

King's College Chapel and colleges to its south

Corpus Christi College, New Court

William Wilkins's reorganisation of Corpus Christi in the early nineteenth century resulted in the college's main entrance being moved from St Bene't's churchyard to Trumpington Street. This gave direct access to Wilkins's New Court, to which Old Court (see page 5.4) henceforth became secondary.

Wilkins placed his new chapel on the site of the college's Tudor chapel, opposite the new gate tower. The chapel, which in 1870 was given a new east end in Early English Gothic by Arthur Blomfield, is set centrally in a symmetrical two-storey screen wall. This conceals to the south a new Master's Lodge, and college offices to the north. The screen wall steps forward at each end to join a new two-storey library in the south range, and in the north range the new first-floor hall and its staircase, the original hall being demoted by Wilkins to act as servery. The remainder of the court contains accommodation on three floors, to which a rather unfortunate mansard attic storey was added in 1920 and 1929.

Wilkins' reputation was founded on his early involvement in the Greek Revival. This was his first building in the Gothic, and he chose Tudor-Gothic for it, the style he was to use the following year at King's College (see page 5.42) to match the chapel. Although Wilkins's four-centred arches and other details are correct, the relentless symmetry and regularity of the scheme with its insistent battlements, and the mechanical quality of the cut ashlar stone, feel more Georgian in spirit, failing somehow to capture the quality of Tudor architecture. Nonetheless, this was reputedly his favourite scheme, and he is buried in the college chapel.

ADDRESS Trumpington Street
ACCESS college open daily, 14.00–16.00; closed May and June

William Wilkins 1823–27

King's College Chapel and colleges to its south

William Wilkins 1823–27

Corpus Christi College, Leckhampton House

Leckhampton House was the first graduate hostel to be built in Cambridge. It is in the spacious grounds of a large house at the end of a long driveway off Grange Road. The accommodation is arranged in two towers, one square in plan and four storeys high, the other rectangular in plan and three storeys high. Each tower contains communal facilities on the ground floor and student rooms on the upper floors. The two towers are set apart but linked by a service core that reads as an echelon of red-brick fins infilled with glass. On the approach to the building the red-brick garden wall appears to transform into the staggered fins, implying a connection between the new building and the existing red brick house.

The most distinctive and important element of this scheme is the architectural treatment of the towers. Leckhampton House was the first of Arup Associates' residential buildings in either Oxford or Cambridge to deploy a precast-concrete exoskeleton. The distinctive motifs such as the tripartite vertical division (base as cloister, middle as repeated bays, top as finial), the bay module determined by room size, the recessed window wall, the chamfered frame corners and the fine white precast concrete frame were later repeated at Boulton House for Trinity Hall (see page 4.100) and at Somerville and St John's Colleges, Oxford.

Unfortunately, the brick fins have attracted unsightly moss growth, but from the garden side the towers are pristine and appear heroic and wonderfully refined despite their age and pioneering nature.

ADDRESS Grange Road, opposite Selwyn College
ACCESS none; visible from the approach road

Arup Associates 1963–64

Corpus Christi College, Leckhampton House

King's College Chapel and colleges to its south

Arup Associates 1963–64

Darwin College, Hall and Residential Building

Darwin College was established as a graduate college in 1964 and it commissioned Howell Killick Partridge and Amis to turn three early nineteenth-century houses and their grounds into a college. HKPA proposed filling the gap between two of the houses with a gatehouse and residential accommodation, and adding a new dining hall linked to the west end of the group. The linear series of distinct units was united by a continuous central corridor that took on the architectural character of each part.

The design of the new residential block was intended to be low key. While respecting the street frontage and height of the adjacent buildings, its use of brick fins, lead-covered spandrel panels and plate-glass bay windows is a distinctive architectural statement in its own right. The design of the dining room is more prosaic. A brick canted-square box is raised to first-floor level on concrete columns and sits rather uncomfortably in a tight gap between the college and the adjacent property. Internally, the non-hierarchical centralised plan is enclosed by fair-faced brick walls and views are directed through a very large window on to the garden. The space is roofed with a natural pine ceiling resting on exposed concrete beams and is crowned by a central roof-light. In both buildings no distinction is made between the architectural language and materials used outside and inside. This unity produces buildings whose aesthetic is directly derived from the process of construction.

ADDRESS Silver Street
ACCESS none; visible from Silver Street and Newnham Road

Howell Killick Partridge and Amis 1964–70

Darwin College, Hall and Residential Building

Howell Killick Partridge and Amis 1964–70

Darwin College, Study Centre

Jeremy Dixon and Edward Jones won the limited competition for a study centre with a proposal that continues the linear nature of Darwin by adding a long thin building which entirely fills a sliver of a site between Silver Street and the River Cam, at the east end of the college.

The building consists of a brick base surmounted by a timber superstructure and a monopitch roof. The low-key elevation to the road rebuilds the pre-existing brick boundary wall adding only a clerestory, eaves line and small, witty timber-clad ventilation tower where the building steps up at the east end. By contrast, the river elevation consists of a brick base surmounted by a timber-and-glass structure that seems to allude to medieval timber buildings.

The small entrance vestibule adjacent to the Old Granary opens into a double-height space lit by a vast window facing the river. The circulation follows the book stacks that hug the curve of the street wall, giving access either into a series of four small computer rooms, or up narrow transverse staircases between them to the first-floor reading area. This is light and airy and commands fine views, through a jettied timber-and-glass balcony, across the water towards the meadows. At the end of the linear route are two seminar rooms and a flat stacked one above the other.

The structure of the building is massive with a central row of paired green oak columns supporting a spine beam which in turn supports rafters spanning across to the external load-bearing walls. Contrasted with but complementing the tough structural timber are the fine oak-veneered built-in bookcases and furniture. The whole is delightful.

ADDRESS Silver Street
ACCESS none; visible from Silver Street and Granta Place

Jeremy Dixon and Edward Jones 1989–93

Jeremy Dixon and Edward Jones 1989–93

Darwin College, Frank Young House

Following the success of their Study Centre (see page 5.12) Jeremy Dixon and Edward Jones designed a block of postgraduate accommodation on a suburban site. Their approach was to replicate the surrounding morphology: that of large houses set back from the road in generous gardens. Thus, from Wordsworth Grove the building appears as a pair of rather austere semidetached brick-built residences sitting behind a high garden wall. The south aspect is towards playing fields and here Dixon and Jones's design is handled in an equally formal but more playful manner. The accommodation extends in two wings projecting from the body of the building to form a three-sided courtyard. A strict symmetry about a central axis gives the building a classical flavour. However, the white-rendered courtyard walls, timber decking, top-floor loggia, white-painted railings and metal windows seem to communicate a witty nautical imagery.

Each house contains 14 study-bedrooms, a kitchen, living room and bathrooms. The study-bedrooms wrap around the communal rooms, which look into the courtyard and face south over the playing fields. They are accessed via rather dark, narrow corridors on each floor, which sadly are separated from the light, lantern-lit staircases. The two distinct houses are cleverly joined at each level through a shared central fire-escape stair, designed to encourage communality.

ADDRESS Wordsworth Grove
ACCESS none; visible from Wordsworth Grove and Newnham Road playing field

Jeremy Dixon and Edward Jones 1995

Darwin College, Frank Young House

Jeremy Dixon and Edward Jones 1995

Downing College

Downing College was founded through the bequest of Sir George Downing and gained its charter in 1800. Classical designs were first obtained from James Wyatt but these were rejected, primarily due to Thomas Hope's insistence on a classical design of greater purity, and further designs were sought. Finally William Wilkins's neo-Grecian scheme was selected. Wilkins was a Cambridge architect and a leading Greek Revivalist. He had travelled widely in Greece and in 1807 published a book on Greek architecture. His designs for Downing are seminal as they mark the stylistic transition in England from neo-Classicism to the purer Greek Revival.

Wilkins's design defied the college typology of closed court, the plan consisting instead of a single large green surrounded by freestanding two-storey ashlar ranges. A Greek propylaeum was to mark the entrance on the north side. Three detached blocks of chambers, terminating at their southern ends with the hall and Master's Lodge, formed the east and west sides, while the library and chapel, with attached Ionic porticos, would have formed the splendid south range. In the event, construction stopped in 1821 when only the hall, Master's Lodge and five of the residential blocks had been completed. Construction started again in 1874 when Edward Middleton Barry completed the east range, and mistakenly filled in the gaps between the blocks. In 1929 Herbert Baker added the rather pompous neo-Georgian three-storey north ranges where Wilkins's propylaeum would have stood, while the chapel with its portico completed the north range in 1953 to designs by A T Scott, Baker's successor.

ADDRESS Regent Street
ACCESS college open daily, daylight hours; closed May and June

W Wilkins 1807–20, E M Barry 1873–76, H Baker 1929–53

King's College Chapel and colleges to its south

W Wilkins 1807–20, E M Barry 1873–76, H Baker 1929–53

Downing College, Senior Combination Room

Tucked around the corner from William Wilkins' Greek Revival pavilion that marks the south-west end of the great courtyard (see page 5.16) is a tiny but poetic modernist pavilion. The pavilion houses the Senior Combination Room, the only visible element of a much larger scheme concealed by the high blank wall that forms its backdrop. The designs involved demolition of the old kitchens, extending Wilkins's hall, and adding new kitchens and college offices. The main body of the accommodation is functional but unremarkable, and the architects lavished all their attention on the pavilion, attempting to make a modernist building that would hold its own against Wilkins' serene and dignified Greek Revival designs.

The SCR is contained in a perfectly square pavilion, which is raised on an extension of the hall plinth, giving it comparable status. Narrowing of the link to the new accommodation at the rear enhances the object nature of the pavilion. The structure consists of a series of paired precast concrete perimeter columns supporting beams and lead-covered roofs, turned up to read as split pediments and concealing a central lantern. The inner row of columns is infilled with sliding glass windows and stone panels. The constructional language is elemental, and recalls the Vitruvian primitive hut, the Greek temple and Wilkins' work at Downing. Hence, a chain of historical references is created. The materials and finishes of the interior reflect the exterior. Unfortunately, the minimalist space makes the heavy mahogany furniture and the portraits of distinguished members of the college look rather incongruous.

ADDRESS Regent Street
ACCESS college open daily, daylight hours; closed May and June

Howell Killick Partridge and Amis 1965–70

Downing College, Senior Combination Room

King's College Chapel and colleges to its south

Howell Killick Partridge and Amis 1965–70

Downing College, Howard Building

The Howard Building was given by the inventor of the Cambridge Diet to provide a lecture room suitable for modest theatrical productions on the first floor, and on the ground floor an annexe to the Junior Combination Room, doubling as a foyer for the theatre. The building is free-standing, and with the 1993–94 construction of the adjacent residential range, also designed by Quinlan Terry, now forms a new court to the rear of William Wilkins' original buildings for the college (see page 5.16).

Unlike Wilkins' elegantly restrained Greek Revival designs, the Howard Building provides a rich feast of Renaissance and mannerist motifs; indeed, some would say that the omelette is over-egged. The north elevation, which despite its appearance is rarely used as the main entrance, has giant Corinthian pilasters of white Portland stone contrasting with a background of buff Ketton stone. Attached columns in the centre frame a baroque doorway and window, and support a small pediment surmounted by urns, while the end bays are rusticated and frame alcoves, as do the end elevations. All is raised on a plinth, the first use of this feature at Downing.

The south elevation is a total contrast. The plinth stops at the corners, and there is a terrace supported by six Doric columns that rise from the ground. This Janus-faced quality can be explained in terms of addressing the adjacent range, but denies the pavilion-like language of the north elevation. Moreover, the main rooms are not, as might be expected, located symmetrically behind the elevations. This means that some of the main windows, instead of serving rooms, are blind.

ADDRESS Regent Street
ACCESS college open daily, daylight hours; closed May and June

Quinlan Terry 1985–87

Downing College, Howard Building

Quinlan Terry 1985–87

Downing College, Library

William Wilkins' proposals for Downing College (see page 5.16) involved a Greek Doric propylaeum as entrance to the college, and a range closing the college to the south containing a chapel and library. Neither was built. Quinlan Terry's library, of ashlar-faced stone, is the first purpose-built library in the college's history, and with its Greek Doric portico by the college's entrance recalls Wilkins' objectives.

The portico was modelled by Terry on the Portico of Augustus in Athens, and is reminiscent of Wilkins' Grange Park, built in 1805–09. But while Grange Park is a temple-shaped building, Terry's portico is placed on the south front of a square block, of two storeys and a basement, the form recommended by the college's library consultant. On the east side is another Greek-style projection containing escape stairs, a lift and service ducts, while in the centre of the pyramidal roof is an octagonal lantern, meant to recall the Tower of the Winds by Andronicus, also in Athens. The rest of the building is simply detailed in a neo-Georgian style in tune with the nearby brick-built Junior Combination Room and Regent Street office block, also designed by Terry for the college.

The interior revolves around a grand sweeping staircase in a two-storey octagonal hall under the lantern. Reading desks are under the perimeter windows, with bookcases arranged rather uncomfortably between them and the octagon. Air handling ducts are concealed in the flat-coffered plaster ceilings, reducing their height. Though opulent, the Georgian styling of the interior is not unlike that of an early twentieth-century municipal library.

ADDRESS Regent Street
ACCESS college open during daylight hours; closed May and June

Quinlan Terry 1992–93

King's College Chapel and colleges to its south

Quinlan Terry 1992–93

Emmanuel College, Brick Building

The Brick Building was the first new accommodation to be added to the medieval and Tudor buildings of Emmanuel College after its foundation on the site of a Dominican priory in 1584. At that time the college was entered axially from Emmanuel Street to the north. Front Court (see page 5.28) was still open to the east, and had not yet been remodelled in response to the construction of Christopher Wren's chapel (see page 5.26). The Brick Building is projected as a wing to the south of Front Court, preserving the openness of the college's layout at that time.

John Westley built, and probably designed, this business-like building, one room deep, of three storeys and an attic, whose purpose was to help house the growing student numbers. There are two staircases, largely original, each serving two rooms on each floor. Each room was to be shared by two students, and consisted of a sleeping area and two screened-off study areas.

The building now appears even more utilitarian than when first constructed. Originally it had Dutch-inspired curved gables at each end (only that to the south remains), and a row of small decorative gables each side, in front of the dormer windows. The present flat-topped dormers are nineteenth century. The chimneys were also more decorative. The doorways retain their stone heads with decorative strapwork carving. By using brick, here heightened with stone dressings, Westley was following in a Cambridge tradition dating at least from the mid-fifteenth century at Queens' College (see page 5.72). However, his next building for Clare College (see page 4.14) was entirely of stone.

ADDRESS St Andrew's Street
ACCESS college open daily, 9.30–18.00; closed May and June

John Westley (bricklayer) 1633–34

John Westley (bricklayer) 1633–34

Emmanuel College, Chapel and Gallery

This, Christopher Wren's second college chapel at Cambridge (the first was started five years earlier at Pembroke College, see page 5.56), was designed in 1666, at the command of William Sancroft, the previous Master, and by then Dean of St Paul's. At that time Front Court (see page 5.28) was still Tudor in appearance, and the classical chapel, which closed it off to the east, presented a striking stylistic contrast.

The arrangement of chapel with linking galleries harked back to that at Peterhouse (see page 5.66), where Wren's uncle had been Master. Wren, however, cleverly disengaged his west front from the chapel proper, allowing the open cloister, and a new long-gallery attached to the Master's Lodge to the north, to pass behind it without interruption.

Compared with the Pembroke chapel, and with the plain walls and arched windows of the chapel's other elevations, Wren's west front is remarkably baroque. It shows the influence of his recent visit to Paris and sets the scene for his later work. In front of the rhythm of identical windows and arches (that in the middle was widened by Robert Grumbold in 1677) and continuous string courses, Wren superimposes full-height corner pilasters and two engaged columns, whose Corinthian capitals are linked by a frieze of garlands. These allow the entablature to step forward in the centre to carry a pedestal, which forces the pediment apart. Above, is a six-sided cupola and elongated dome.

The chapel is entered from the cloister through an antechapel below the organ gallery. The interior, fitted out in 1676–77, has a sumptuous plastered ceiling, and oak pews, panelling and an altarpiece designed by Edward Pierce and John Oliver of London.

ADDRESS St Andrew's Street
ACCESS college open daily, 9.30–18.00; closed May and June

Christopher Wren 1668–73

Emmanuel College, Chapel and Gallery

King's College Chapel and colleges to its south

Christopher Wren 1668–73

5.28

Emmanuel College, Front Court

Before Christopher Wren's chapel (see page 5.26) closed in its east side in 1673, Front Court consisted of two ranges of the original medieval priory buildings, converted to college use, on the north and west sides, and to the south the Founder's Building, completed c.1587. These were all rebuilt or remodelled over the next century in the classical style.

In 1719–22 the Founder's Building was rebuilt on a deeper floor plan to provide a grand showpiece opposite the main college entrance, which was then from Emmanuel Street to the north. Named the Westmorland Building after the 6th Earl, it is a three-storey ashlar-faced building with tall regularly spaced sash windows with keystones, and a parapet. The central three bays are flanked by giant Ionic pilasters, reminiscent of Thomas Archer's designs, and are further emphasised by a balustrade with urns, and the family arms of the earl mounted over the doorway. Its designer is unknown.

Then, in 1760–64, the north range was remodelled by James Essex. Essex refitted the hall, adding fine panelling and a plaster ceiling below the sixteenth-century open timber roof. He also refaced the south elevation in ashlar stonework, replaced the windows with sash windows and gave the roof regularly spaced pedimented dormers.

Finally, in 1769–75 the medieval range facing St Andrew's Street was rebuilt to classical designs by Essex, and the college given its present main entrance opposite the chapel. Here, two three-storey pavilions flank a two-storey range. These consist of the end wall of the Westmorland Building, and a matching block by Essex to the north. Inside the court Essex echoed Wren's cloister with an open arcade.

ADDRESS St Andrew's Street
ACCESS college open daily, 9.30–18.00; closed May and June

1719–22, James Essex 1760–64, 1769–75

King's College Chapel and colleges to its south

1719–22, James Essex 1760–64, 1769–75

Emmanuel College, South Court

The commissions for the residential South Court and the Master's Lodge (1963–64) were made under Edward Welbourne, then Master, and awarded on the strength of Hancock's work at Priory Mews, Wallingford.

South Court consists of two three-storey residential ranges, running slightly askew, linked by a low common-room block with a roof terrace at the north end. The north elevation, which forms the south range to Chapman's Garden, is cleverly composed so that the ends of the two residential ranges extend beyond the central common-room block to form porticos under which the route from Front Court to New Garden passes, thus locking the new building into the pre-existing circulation pattern. Great care has been taken to follow the scale and materials of the surrounding buildings yet the style is uncompromising in its modernist language. A clear reference to Le Corbusier's Maisons Jaoul, Neuilly-sur-Seine, near Paris (1955–57), is seen in the use of fixed glazing flanked by copper-clad opening flaps.

The arrangement of the residential ranges has great clarity. A wide ground-floor cloister looking into the internal court leads to a series of bold semicircular top-lit staircases that serve groups of rooms above. On the upper floors the rooms are double-banked allowing both elevations to consist entirely of repeated student rooms. South Court is quintessentially a building of its time and, as with Basil Spence's Erasmus Building (see page 5.80), the architectural language is reticent and refined. South Court deserves attention for its studied response to brief and context.

ADDRESS St Andrew's Street
ACCESS college open daily, 9.30–18.00; closed May and June

Tom Hancock 1962–66

King's College Chapel and colleges to its south

Tom Hancock 1962–66

Emmanuel College, Queen's Building

The Mastership of Lord St John of Fawsley, an apologist for modern architecture, may explain the selection of Michael Hopkins and Partners as architects for this auditorium. The building, a box with apsidal ends, sits as a freestanding object on a triangular site away from the heart of the college, but on an important route from the main college buildings, through the subway under Emmanuel Street, to North Court.

The limestone shell of the building is divided by fine shadow gaps into a tartan grid of load-bearing prestressed columns, which reduce in width at each storey. The windows are without reveals and complete the sheer, taut skin of the building.

The plan is symmetrical on the long axis and very restrained. The ground floor contains cellular rooms surrounded by an open colonnade. Access to the larger volumes on the upper floors is via an entrance lobby located off a passage which runs through the building. Vertical circulation is by an enclosed spiral staircase, which provides the visitor with a sense of release when entering the spacious upper level. Here, the double-height auditorium takes up two-thirds of the plan, and has an apsidal performance space, with raked seating and a narrow perimeter balcony. Its spatial qualities are reminiscent both of Hopkins' Glyndebourne Opera House, Sussex (1989–94) and Christopher Wren's Sheldonian Theatre, Oxford. The use of timber for the walls, seats and ceiling provides the space with a feeling of warmth and richness that contrasts wonderfully with the severe stone cladding of the exterior shell.

ADDRESS St Andrew's Street, Emmanuel Street
ACCESS college open daily, 9.30–18.00; closed May and June

Michael Hopkins and Partners 1993–95

Emmanuel College, Queen's Building

Michael Hopkins and Partners 1993–95

Gonville and Caius College, Harvey Court

Nearly 40 years after its conception the form of Harvey Court seems to sum up the theoretical preoccupations of the 1960s – structural rationalism, perimeter development and truth to materials. This courtyard development of some 100 student rooms was designed to be extended by a further courtyard to the south, which was never realised.

From Grange Road the building reads as a defensive, almost castle-like form. The façade is articulated by a series of brick piers that support a blank top storey and form a double-height arcade around the perimeter. Further articulation is provided at irregular intervals by brick enclosures that follow the paths of staircases – a quotation from Alvar Aalto's MIT Dormitory in Boston, Massachusetts (1947–48). The monolithic-seeming block is in fact a perimeter strip of student rooms wrapped around a raised first-floor courtyard, under which are the common facilities. The enclosure is broken for the entrance on the east side. On the south side broad steps leading down from the courtyard to the garden are reminiscent of Aalto's Säynätsalo Town Hall (1949–52). The student study-bedrooms look into the empty court, apart from those on the south side which face the gardens. The stepped-back section on three levels provides all the rooms with balconies and, together with the expressive cross-wall construction, produces a strongly modulated façade. The main horizontal circulation is on the courtyard level where broad 'internal streets', side-lit from slot windows in the perimeter wall, give access to staircases feeding the groups of student rooms. The atmosphere is one of calm monastic contemplation signified by a highly controlled aesthetic.

ADDRESS Grange Road
ACCESS none; visible from the street

Leslie Martin in association with Colin St John Wilson 1960–62

King's College Chapel and colleges to its south

Leslie Martin in association with Colin St John Wilson 1960–62

King's College, Chapel

Henry VI founded King's College in 1441. The king set down his intentions for the plan of his college: the chapel was to be in its present location, with a spacious court adjoining it to the south.

Construction of the chapel took nearly 70 years, covering four reigns, but stayed true to the plan whose walls were set out at the start by Reginald Ely, the first master mason. Building started in 1446 at the east end. By c.1485 the first five bays were roofed over and were in use. Henry VII initiated the chapel's completion between 1508 and 1515, which was overseen by his executors after his death in 1509.

The chapel – a huge single light-filled volume of 12 bays – is divided internally into antechapel and chapel by a screen (see page 5.38), and flanked by low side chapels and two porches between the stepping buttresses. It is in the Perpendicular Gothic, a style promoted at Westminster, Windsor and Eton by the Court. Henry VI's work, though magnificent, is understated, but by Henry VII's time the buttresses and the interior of the antechapel were embellished with finely carved symbols of royal patronage.

John Wastell was the master mason who from 1508 saw the building to completion, and the wide west window, the four corner stair turrets, buttress pinnacles and pierced battlements are his. The roof of the chapel was intended to have a complex lierne vault, but from c.1480 the idea of a stone fan vault divided into bays by four-centred arches was decided on, and Wastell, with Henry Semark, built this from 1512 to 1515.

ADDRESS King's Parade; entrance from Trinity Lane
ACCESS chapel open term time Monday to Saturday, 9.30–15.30; vacations Monday to Saturday, 9.30–16.30; Sunday, 10.00–17.00; admission charge

1446–1515

King's College Chapel and colleges to its south

1446–1515

King's College Chapel, Screen and Fittings

Once the shell of King's College Chapel (see page 5.36) was complete, the college initiated the glazing of the windows, using a team working initially under Barnard Flowers, the king's glazier. The scheme, completed by 1531, depicts Old Testament subjects above, with their New Testament parallels below; messengers with scrolls occupy the middle lights. The east window depicts the Crucifixion; the glass of the west window is from 1879. The Renaissance style of the architectural settings depicted in the windows contrasts with the Perpendicular Gothic design of the chapel.

The same is true of the substantial oak screen, given by Henry VIII, and built in 1533–36 in the place and of the depth originally specified by Henry VI. A group of Italian artists had made the Renaissance tomb of Henry VII at Westminster Abbey in 1512–18, but it is not known who built the King's screen. However, the semicircular arches, flat pilasters and decorations are typical of Italian work of the time, and are unique in England. The screen doors, in a matching style, are dated 1636.

The organ designed in 1688 by René Harris now incorporates the choir organ of 1661 on the east face of the screen. In 1859 George Gilbert Scott added the angels, based on a 1690 engraving. The stalls were built in 1536–38 in a style similar to the screen; the balusters, cornice and coats of arms of the upper stalls were added in 1633. The altar and its setting have been redesigned many times. The present arrangement was designed by Martyn Beckett to provide a setting for Rubens' *Adoration of the Magi* (1634).

ADDRESS King's Parade; entrance from Trinity Lane
ACCESS chapel open term time Monday to Saturday, 9.30–15.30; vacations Monday to Saturday, 9.30–16.30; Sunday, 10.00–17.00; admission charge

1515–36 and later

1515–36 and later

King's College, Fellows' Building

In 1713 Nicholas Hawksmoor produced plans for completing Henry VI's court (see page 5.36) with three ranges of new buildings. At the same time he made a sketch proposal for rebuilding the centre of Cambridge along classical lines (see Introduction) of which his proposals for King's College formed an important part. Despite a redesign, the scheme seemed to the Provost, Dr John Adams, too grand and ambitious.

In 1724 James Gibbs, working on the Senate House (see page 3.4), was approached for something plainer. As at the Senate House, he proposed three ranges to form a court. The east range contained the entrance, the south range the hall, and the west range chambers. Only the west range was built to Gibbs's design, and is less ornate than proposed.

The white Portland stone and classical horizontality of the Fellows' Building, also known as the Gibbs's Building, is in striking contrast with the Gothic chapel. The base is rusticated, the upper two floors have smooth walling with accentuated first-floor windows, and there is a balustraded parapet. The east elevation has 23 bays, while that to the west has only 17 in response to the internal layout of the rooms, which are served by four staircases. The middle three bays of both main elevations, on axis with the then position of the bridge, step forward and enclose a Doric portico. This is surmounted by a pediment, a semicircular window and swags, and a further pediment level with the balustrade, the whole giving the building a monumental, somewhat mannerist, central emphasis. The building was more costly than anticipated and consequently the other two ranges were never started.

ADDRESS King's Parade
ACCESS college open Monday to Saturday, 9.00–16.30; Sunday, 10.00–17.00; admission charge

James Gibbs 1724–49

King's College Chapel and colleges to its south

James Gibbs 1724–49

King's College, Front Court

Following the completion in 1749 of James Gibbs's Fellows' Building (see page 5.40) King's College commissioned Robert Adam in 1784 and then James Wyatt in 1795 to produce schemes to complete Front Court. Finally, in 1822, William Wilkins won a competition for the commission.

In 1807 Wilkins had distinguished himself in Cambridge with his Greek designs for Downing College (see page 5.16), and in 1819 had worked for King's College designing the new bridge and gate piers to Queen's Road in the classical style. In 1823–25 he had designed New Court at Trinity College (see page 4.92) in Tudor style, and following Wyatt's lead and the style of the chapel he chose this for his winning scheme at King's. He also proposed to remodel Gibbs's Fellows' Building to match.

Wilkins cleverly proposed a pierced screen with a central gatehouse to face King's Parade when the intervening buildings were cleared away, leaving the south elevation of the chapel entirely open to view. Wilkins's screen echoes the four-centred arches, pinnacles and turrets of the chapel, although he used a lierne vault above the gateway. Opposite the chapel he designed an asymmetrical range consisting of the hall, flanked by three storeys of chambers. The hall, whose entrance has been relocated from the west end, and whose lanterns were redesigned in 1952, has a fine four-centred timber ceiling with pendants, and linenfold panelling in the Tudor style. To the west of this Wilkins added a two-storey secondary range with the library on the first floor and the Provost's Lodge beyond, into which the library has now been extended.

ADDRESS King's Parade
ACCESS college open Monday to Saturday, 9.00–16.30; Sunday, 10.00–17.00; admission charge

William Wilkins 1824–28

William Wilkins 1824–28

King's College, King's Lane Development

In 1963 Fello Atkinson and James Cubitt and Partners were asked to prepare a comprehensive redevelopment plan for the dingy and depressing area which formed the boundary between St Catherine's and King's Colleges. The development was considered remarkable at the time as it appeared to be the first time that two colleges had actually collaborated on a building project.

The delicate Gothic-like stone-and-bronze bay that protrudes into Trumpington Street belies the magnitude of this scheme. The realigned King's Lane passes through the middle of a complex network of four new courts and ranges that house mixed residential and communal rooms, including a new hall and kitchens for St Catherine's College. A later brick boundary wall largely obscures the two St Catherine's courts, but the rather drearily landscaped King's Chetwynd Court is visible through pilotis to the north. Internally the accommodation is disappointingly dark and spatially undistinguished, and the circulation labyrinthine.

The new buildings may be seamlessly tied into the pre-existing buildings on plan, but aesthetically they take on uncompromisingly modernist styling. The white limestone-clad façades with their strip windows and pilotis are derived from Le Corbusier's early work. Nonetheless, the scale of the pieces and the composition of the façades coexist comfortably with the historic context. This is particularly true of the finely worked bay to King's Parade which, although perhaps a little mannered, sits happily with its Georgian and Gothic neighbours.

ADDRESS King's Parade, King's Lane
ACCESS none; visible from King's Parade and King's Lane

Fello Atkinson and James Cubitt and Partners 1965–68

King's College Chapel and colleges to its south

Fello Atkinson and James Cubitt and Partners 1965–68

Newnham College

Newnham College was founded in 1874. It aimed to provide a liberal education for women in informal surroundings not far from the city centre, and Champneys' relaxed and creative architecture is a pleasant contrast with that provided by Alfred Waterhouse at Girton College (see page 4.30). Champneys started by building Newnham Hall (now renamed Old Hall) in 1874–75, and followed this in 1879–80 with North Hall (now renamed Sidgwick Hall). When Sidgwick Avenue was laid out in 1891 the closure of the road that ran through the site allowed the pattern of large freestanding houses, informally related to each other around a garden, to continue during his long association with the college.

Champneys was one of a number of architects, including Richard Norman Shaw and John J Stephenson, who created a style of architecture based on a revival of the early eighteenth-century Queen Anne period. Stephenson designed several houses in Cambridge (for example in Selwyn Gardens), but Champneys' work at Newnham is easily Cambridge's best example of the 'Queen Anne' style.

The college is best approached down Newnham Walk, through the red-brick gatehouse (1892–93) with its white-painted timber windows, Dutch-style gable and studiedly asymmetrical turrets with copper roofs. The theme of the college buildings is red brickwork and terracotta, with projecting gabled bays and decorative carving, contrasting with white painted cornices, dormers, lanterns, roof balustrading and a variety of window shapes and sizes, among which the bay windows of the dining hall (part of Clough Hall, 1886–87) are the finest.

ADDRESS Sidgwick Avenue
ACCESS apply at porter's lodge

Basil Champneys 1874–1910

Basil Champneys 1874–1910

Newnham College, Katherine Stephen Room

This small but monumental barrel-vaulted building, standing assertively in the ragged margins between Sidgwick Avenue and Basil Champneys' nineteenth-century college buildings, offers the visitor little clue to its *raison d'être*. However, the jewel-box-like form enclosed by banded brickwork suggests that it may contain something of value. It is no surprise, therefore, that the building was conceived as a container for Newnham College's collection of rare books as part of a strategy to expand the college's library provision.

The building is the second addition to Champneys' original library of 1896. The first was the adjacent 1960s addition by Christopher Grillet through which the new rare books room is entered via a small oval lobby in the south-west corner. Whereas Grillet's work makes no architectural reference to the surrounding buildings, the new building consciously alludes to Champneys' library by replicating its barrel-vaulted central nave and light mezzanine structure. However, the architectural form and detailing is much simpler. Here the barrel-vaulted exterior echoes the interior volume. A clear distinction is made between container and contained: the permanent brick skin (concealing a steel-framed structure) contains a flexible lining of metal shelving and a mezzanine level. The barrel-vaulted space is lit by a skylight running along its length, which provides a warm, soft quality of light. Apart from alluding to Champneys' original library, the delicate interior recalls both Pierre-François-Henri Labrouste's Bibliothèque Ste-Geneviève in Paris and the library of Otto Wagner's Post Office Building in Vienna.

ADDRESS Sidgwick Avenue
ACCESS none; visible from the street

Van Heyningen and Haward 1983

Newnham College, Katherine Stephen Room

King's College Chapel and colleges to its south

Van Heyningen and Haward 1983

Newnham College, Rosalind Franklin Building

This accommodation block for graduate students sits apart from the main college group and takes the form of a linear block spanning between Sidgwick Avenue and Newnham Lane. The barn-like building contains five 'houses', each with two one-bedroom flats at ground level and eight study-bedrooms and associated communal rooms above. Access to the flats and units above is from through-passages which link a new lane to the east of the block with the Graduate Garden to its west, on the college side.

The building is of two storeys, with generous dormers lighting a third floor. The red brickwork of the walls and white-painted woodwork are chosen to match Basil Champneys' work in the main parts of the college (see page 5.46). Where the passages face the lane their entrances are small and low, and marked by a white-rendered wall. On the side facing the Graduate Garden and the college they open up and enclose white-painted balconies that serve the first-floor common rooms. The architectural language continues that employed by the architects at Sarum Hall School, London (1995). The envelope is detailed as a series of layers to suggest a tough brick envelope which, when peeled away, reveals a more delicate white interior. The use of a restricted palate of materials, the simple detailing of wall, window and balcony, together with a skilful handling of proportions and elevational composition, combine to make this building a successful essay in contextual modernism.

ADDRESS Sidgwick Avenue, Newnham Lane
ACCESS none; visible from Sidgwick Avenue and Newnham Walk

Allies and Morrison 1995

Newnham College, Rosalind Franklin Building

King's College Chapel and colleges to its south

Allies and Morrison 1995

Pembroke College, First Court

Pembroke College was founded in 1347 and built in 1351–98. The college then consisted of just the small northern half of First Court. This was closed by a range to the south, the end of which is today marked by a stone gable. This south range was demolished in 1874 to give First Court its present enlarged size. The west and north ranges date from the mid-fourteenth century, and although entirely refaced in 1712–17 their Gothic windows and doorways are largely medieval in appearance.

The college's modest entrance is below two oriel windows that, although rebuilt, appear to be fourteenth century. To its left was the original mid-fourteenth-century chapel, the first to be built from new as part of a Cambridge college. This was remodelled as a library in 1690, and its north-facing brickwork, windows and fine plaster ceiling are all of that date. The original hall occupied the range opposite the entrance, and in 1452 a library with attic rooms above was built on top of it. The kitchens were to its north, and to its south was the Combination Room. The Master's Lodge was next to this. In 1875 the hall was replaced and enlarged by Alfred Waterhouse in a Victorian Gothic style. Further storeys were added when the hall was remodelled in 1925.

In 1664 the court was linked to Christopher Wren's new chapel (see page 5.56) by Hitcham's Cloister. This extended the college's Trumpington Street elevation in a uniform medieval style, but presented a classical arcaded cloister to the small court thus formed to the north of the chapel. In 1880 the arcade was lengthened by a bay at each end and partly enclosed, and, like Wren's chapel, had its original stucco removed to expose the red brick construction.

ADDRESS Trumpington Street
ACCESS college open daily, daylight hours; closed May to mid-June

Fourteenth century and later

Pembroke College, Ivy Court

Ivy Court was the first extension to Pembroke after the college's construction in the mid-fourteenth century (see page 5.52). The first two-thirds of the north range were built in 1614–17, and the range was completed by Robert Grumbold in the same style in 1670. The south range, known as Hitcham Building, was begun in 1659 in a similar style. A wall enclosed the east side of the open court, with gates leading to the Fellows' Garden.

The north range set the style that the rest of Ivy Court followed, although after the rebuilding of its dormer windows the south range is now a better guide to its original appearance. Two storeys of simple stone mullioned windows are set in brick walls with gabled dormers above, similar to those in the 1598–1602 Second Court of St John's College (see page 4.66). There were smaller garrets in the steep roof above these.

The first four bays of the south range were given a more distinctive treatment, probably as part of the then adjacent Master's Lodge. They are attributed to Peter Mills, who with Christopher Wren became a surveyor to the City of London, and whose best-known work is Thorpe Hall, near Peterborough (1653–54). The windows have stone cross-shaped mullions and transoms, and the central pair are linked by arches and surmounted by a pediment. The attic above has a prominent stone segmental pediment, flanked by triangular pediments. By 1663 this dated 'artisan mannerism' was to be put in the shade by Wren's new chapel (see page 5.56), for which full-size detailed wall paintings have been discovered inside the building.

ADDRESS Trumpington Street
ACCESS college open daily, daylight hours; closed May to mid-June

1614–17, Peter Mills 1659

King's College Chapel and colleges to its south

1614–17, Peter Mills 1659

Pembroke College, Chapel

Pembroke College's new chapel was the gift of Matthew Wren, Fellow of the college and Bishop of Ely, the result of a vow made during his imprisonment in the Tower of London. Christopher Wren, his nephew, was then Savilian Professor of Astronomy at Oxford, and this was his first completed building. It is Cambridge's first classical building, and predates Wren's Emmanuel College chapel (see page 5.26) by five years.

The chapel, originally intended to be freestanding, is a rectangular temple-like volume of four bays under a shallow roof, expressed at each end as a pediment. The west elevation is modelled on Sebastiano Serlio's reconstruction of the temple by the river at Tivoli, illustrated in his *Five Books of Architecture* (1537; published in English in 1611). Four Corinthian pilasters support a deep entablature below the pediment, which is enriched with a cartouche and garlands. The roof sports flaming urns and an unorthodox hexagonal timber cupola. The east elevation has a three-light window, again taken from Serlio.

Inside, the organ case dates from 1707, but the pavement, oak antechapel, panelling and stalls are all original, as are the cushions. Above the panelling Wren's walls and coved ceiling are richly decorated with carved plasterwork.

In 1880 George Gilbert Scott Jr restored the chapel and extended it one bay east to provide for a sanctuary. Scott reused the stonework of Wren's east wall, but inexplicably decided to remove the render from the side walls to expose the underlying red brickwork. Inside, his opulent High Victorian Gothic sanctuary, framed by marble columns, seems at odds with Wren's classical interior.

ADDRESS Trumpington Street
ACCESS college open daily, daylight hours; closed May to mid-June

Christopher Wren 1663–65, George Gilbert Scott Jr 1880

King's College Chapel and colleges to its south

Christopher Wren 1663–65, George Gilbert Scott Jr 1880

Pembroke College, Red Building

Alfred Waterhouse designed widely at Cambridge. In addition to his work at Pembroke there are buildings of his at The Union Society, at Gonville and Caius College (see page 4.40), at Jesus College, at Trinity Hall and at Girton College (see page 4.30). He also designed Foster's (now Lloyds) Bank in Sidney Street. Waterhouse has been criticised for being unresponsive to the historic context of Cambridge, yet his buildings exude confidence, creativity and technical competence, and are a lasting monument to the High Victorian period.

At Pembroke his proposals for a new chapel with a campanile to replace Christopher Wren's (see page 5.56) were fortunately rejected, but he did build a group of new buildings including the Master's Lodge in 1871, the Red Building, a new hall and the library, before being dismissed in 1878.

The Red Building, designed as undergraduates' rooms, finds little contextual resonance in Trumpington Street, and the stone screen linking it to the chapel is weak. However, its rich detailing, studied asymmetry and massing, rising from two storeys by the chapel to three at the south end, make it a good addition to the street. The depressed arches, steep roofs, gables and dormers, fretted balustrade and particularly the tower facing the court belong to the French early-Renaissance style. Waterhouse's inventiveness is shown in his choice of a polychromatic palette of green slate, red brick, buff stone and black paintwork. His handling of the wall surface, where random-length quoins are extended as stone bands against a field of precisely detailed brickwork, has an almost abstract quality.

ADDRESS Trumpington Street
ACCESS college open daily, daylight hours; closed May to mid-June

Alfred Waterhouse 1871–72

Pembroke College, Red Building

Alfred Waterhouse 1871–72

Pembroke College, New Building

By the late nineteenth century the Fellows of Pembroke had grown tired of Alfred Waterhouse's grandiose ideas for the college. So it was no great surprise that they abandoned Waterhouse, and the design of the residential New Court went to George Gilbert Scott Jr, already known in Cambridge for his 1870 remodelling of the hall at Peterhouse (see page 5.64).

The New Building lies to the east of Waterhouse's Master's Lodge. An L-shaped range of three storeys encloses a court open to the college garden to the south, and which to the north forms the boundary to Pembroke Street. The design consists of an eclectic mix of details drawn from sixteenth- to eighteenth-century English architecture in a manner similar to T G Jackson's recently completed Examination Schools at Oxford. Nikolaus Pevsner suggested that Scott's main inspiration might have been the Fellows' Building at Christ's College (see page 4.4). Examples of his eclecticism include the Gibbs surrounds to the ground-floor windows, the Arts and Crafts carved grotesques and plants in the entrance arch, the large seventeenth-century first-floor windows with their stone mullions and transoms, and the curiously pedimented Dutch gables to the dormer windows. Despite the jumble of references Scott, made a composition which is at once varied and controlled.

The matching link between Scott's New Building and Waterhouse's Master's Lodge, the brick building to the west and the baroque arched stone screen to Pembroke Street were all designed by W D Carōe and built in 1907.

ADDRESS Trumpington Street, Pembroke Street
ACCESS college open daily, daylight hours; closed May to mid-June

George Gilbert Scott Jr 1879

Pembroke College, New Building

King's College Chapel and colleges to its south

George Gilbert Scott Jr 1879

Pembroke College, New Residences

Eric Parry's 1998 feasibility study for the expansion of Pembroke College suggested the creation of a three-sided court on the far south-east corner of the college grounds, then occupied by Maurice Webb's 1933 Master's Lodge. The fairly uninspiring lodge was duly demolished and replaced by an L-shaped court, housing student accommodation and a replacement Master's Lodge, whose form followed the existing college pattern of partly closed courts.

The restraint of the ranges facing the college contrasts with the street frontage, where wings and courts are added to take up the slack between the building and the street. The front/back distinction displayed by the plan is evident in the elevational treatment. The architectural language is based on a regular stone-clad frame infilled with panels of stone and glass. On the college side the frame is expressed by recessing the infill panels, while on the road elevation the infill is brought into the same plane as the frame. The exception is the elevation to the Master's Lodge, where the plain wall has conventional sash windows, and the living room an applied bay window with a balcony above.

Unusually for Cambridge the student rooms are arranged either side of a corridor. The main staircase and entrance lie at the cruck of the 'L' and are marked by a delicate glass lantern designed by Peter Aldridge. The staircases, corridors and rooms have elegantly designed fittings and details which add a layer of delicacy and finesse to the carefully controlled shell of the building.

ADDRESS Trumpington Street, Tennis Court Lane
ACCESS college open daily, daylight hours; closed May to mid-June

Eric Parry Architects 1995–97

King's College Chapel and colleges to its south

Eric Parry Architects 1995–97

Peterhouse, Old Court

The foundation of Peterhouse by Hugh de Balsham, Bishop of Ely, dates from 1280, making it the first Cambridge college. Its statutes were modelled on Merton College, Oxford, founded just ten years earlier. For the first years of the college's existence the scholars occupied two hostels in Trumpington Street. The first of the college's new buildings was the hall of 1286, which now forms the south side of Old Court. It was heightened in the fifteenth century and heavily restored in the nineteenth century by George Gilbert Scott Jr, leaving little of the original. The interior has a tiled fireplace and stained glass by Morris & Co. The other ranges are fifteenth century, the north residential range dating from 1424 to 1425, the Old Library and the west range from 1430 to 1431, and the Combination Room and Master's Lodge from 1460 to 1464. The east range was formed by the irregular backs of the medieval hostels, until the chapel (see page 5.66) replaced them in the seventeenth century. The north wall of the north range, seen from the adjacent churchyard, gives an impression of the character of the fifteenth-century buildings.

With the exception of the hall, Old Court now appears entirely eighteenth-century neo-Palladian in character – the result of James Burrough's refacing of 1754–56. Burrough, amateur architect and academic, built Peterhouse's Burrough's Building in 1738–42 (see page 5.68) and was responsible for the refacing of many other medieval college buildings. Burrough's work here is rather dull and restrained. The ranges have two-storey ashlar fronts with attics, the only accent being the plain pediment on the west range.

ADDRESS Trumpington Street
ACCESS college open daily, 10.00–17.00; closed May and June

Thirteenth century, James Burrough 1754–56

King's College Chapel and colleges to its south

Thirteenth century, James Burrough 1754–56

Peterhouse, Chapel

Peterhouse was founded in 1280 but was without its own chapel until 1632. The construction of a college chapel was part of a larger scheme to remove the medieval hostels on the Trumpington Street frontage and to erect a new court, First Court (1628–33), between the street and Old Court. First Court is highly memorable because of its open side to the street and the centrally placed chapel with its flanking colonnades. The designer of the chapel is unknown but the mason was George Thompson.

The simple rectangular chapel was built of brick, but faced in ashlar in the late seventeenth century. The entrance façade in Old Court is an extraordinarily elaborate affair. The ground floor is subdivided into bays by depressed blank arcades. The whole elevation is rusticated and contains a central three-light Perpendicular window flanked by niches with ogee tops. This is crowned by a spectacular curvy gable with a raised centre. The flanking colonnades were originally Gothic in style but were remodelled to a more classical design in the early eighteenth century. The east end was refaced in 1665 with rather more restraint than the west end: a plain ashlar façade is flanked by octagonal turrets and contains a five-light Perpendicular window flanked by niches. The crowning motif is a restrained pediment.

The interior has a single-storey antechapel divided from the body of the chapel by the original seventeenth-century screen. The finely decorated cambered timber ceiling and stalls are also original but heavily restored. The reredos and altar rails are eighteenth century.

ADDRESS Trumpington Street
ACCESS college open daily, 10.00–17.00; closed May and June

George Thompson (mason) 1628–32

George Thompson (mason) 1628–32

Peterhouse, Burrough's Building

In 1733 the college decided to replace the seventeenth-century north range of Front Court. James Burrough prepared designs in 1736 and construction started in 1738. Burrough, like George Clarke at Oxford, was an academic with an amateur interest in architecture. He acted as adviser for many of the early eighteenth-century buildings in Cambridge and was responsible for much of the refacing work, including Old Court for Peterhouse (see page 5.64). Here he designed a building from new, and after Clare College chapel (see page 4.18) it is his best.

The building is in a restrained neo-Palladian manner, a style somewhat indebted to James Gibbs but without the baroque flourishes. It is a rectangular three-storey ashlar range with cellars. The primary façade of seven bays faces Front Court and has a central entrance, a heavily rusticated base, tall windows with bracketed sills, and alternating round and pedimented hoods to the principal floor. The upper storey has smaller square-headed windows, a projecting cornice and a balustraded parapet. The language of the south façade is repeated on the east elevation. However, the addition of a ground-floor niche, a first-floor Venetian window with Ionic pilasters and a rooftop pediment with a tympanum containing a cartouche flanked by palms gives it an appropriately stately presence on the street. The minor north façade, facing the adjacent church, is of white brick and is plainly detailed. The interior has a central hall and staircase flanked by large rooms with fireplaces. Most of the original internal panelling, ceilings and fittings remain.

ADDRESS Trumpington Street
ACCESS college open daily, 10.00–17.00; closed May and June

James Burrough 1738–42

King's College Chapel and colleges to its south

James Burrough 1738–42

Peterhouse, William Stone Building

In the 1960s Leslie Martin and Colin St John Wilson taught at the Cambridge School of Architecture and were arguably the most prominent establishment architects of the period. Their residential building for Peterhouse is remarkable for its blatant rejection of all Cambridge typological and morphological precedent and is a mark of 1960s' self assurance: the replacement of the old and outmoded with the relevant new.

The eight-storey block containing 24 undergraduate rooms and eight Fellows' rooms stands near the southern end of Peterhouse's garden, close to St Peter's Terrace. The plan has five rooms per floor arranged in echelon on the west side, with a block of interlocking towers containing a service core and lift on the east side. The open façade facing the garden consists of stepped bands of glazing alternating with bands of brickwork and is in contrast with the monolithic brickwork of the east façade. Between the rooms and the service blocks is a generous reverse echelon landing opening out to a window seat, which gives views north towards the college. The inset entrance slides between the lift tower and the body of the building and its position is marked by the stepping of the plinth. The structure is of load-bearing brickwork with concrete floor slabs throughout.

The detailing is as thorough and self-assured as at Martin and Wilson's earlier Harvey Court (see page 5.34). Here again the debt to Alvar Aalto (this time his brick Pensions Institute in Helsinki, 1952–56) and Louis Kahn's concepts of 'served and serviced' spaces is pronounced.

ADDRESS Trumpington Street
ACCESS college open daily, 10.00–17.00; closed May and June

Leslie Martin and Colin St John Wilson 1963–64

Peterhouse, William Stone Building

King's College Chapel and colleges to its south

Leslie Martin and Colin St John Wilson 1963–64

Queens' College, Front Court

Queens' College was refounded in 1448 by Margaret of Anjou, Henry VI's Queen. Front Court, the original building, was completed within a couple of years, and it is assumed that the designer was Reginald Ely, the King's master mason, who was at that time engaged at King's College Chapel (see page 5.36). The buildings are described by the Royal Commission on Historical Monuments as 'among the best-preserved examples of medieval collegiate architecture in the University'.

The court was originally bounded on three sides by lanes that determined its size and shape. The building, of two storeys with attics, is faced with brick, possibly imported from The Netherlands, and has stone dressings. Small battlemented towers stand at each corner, and the entrance is through a gate tower with octagonal corner turrets, which retains its original gates and stone ribbed vault. The hall, with its bay window, is opposite, with the President's Lodge originally to its north and the kitchens to its south. The original chapel, now a library, is in the north range with a gable to the street, with the library on the first floor to its west. The other ranges contained sets of rooms accessed from staircases, with their tall chimney stacks, now rebuilt, on the outside.

The hall was remodelled in 1732–34 to designs by James Burrough, whose gallery, screen and panelling in the classical style remain. The original open timber roof was again revealed in 1845–46. In 1861 George Frederick Bodley employed William Morris to decorate the original fireplace using tiles by Ford Madox Brown, and in 1875 to decorate the walls and roof, supposedly in the original colours.

ADDRESS Queens' Lane
ACCESS college open daily, 13.45–16.30, also 10.15–12.45 July to September; admission charge

Attributed to Reginald Ely (master mason) 1447–49

King's College Chapel and colleges to its south

Attributed to Reginald Ely (master mason) 1447–49

Queens' College, Cloister Court

The freestanding west range of Cloister Court was started soon after 1448 when Front Court (see page 5.72) was still under construction. Like Front Court it is of two storeys with attics and of red brick, with similar Tudor windows. It rises sheer out of the River Cam, which was used to drain latrines behind a gable at the north end, beside the oriel window that dates from 1711 or earlier. A cloistered walk faces the garden, and in 1494–95 further single-storey cloisters were added to form a court cloistered on three sides. In 1564 the range was extended southwards along the river, where Pump Court (see page 5.76) now stands.

About 1540, or perhaps later, a wider two-storey timber-framed gallery was built on top of the north cloister to serve the President's Lodge. Inside, the first-floor gallery is lined for its full length with late sixteenth- or early seventeenth-century panelling with Doric pilasters, and has a plaster ceiling added in 1923 in imitation of one at Haddon Hall, Derbyshire. The elevation facing the court is symmetrical, with projecting pedimented windows, and bay windows in the centre and at each end. These originally extended up as octagonal turrets with stepped pointed roofs terminating in tall weather vanes, but these were removed in the eighteenth century. Originally, too, the walls were plastered over to give a smooth finish, but this was removed in 1911 when the oak posts were added under the turrets, giving the elevation its present 'half-timbered' appearance. Nikolaus Pevsner has with good reason described this as 'the most cheerful and perhaps the most loveable of all Cambridge courts'.

ADDRESS Queens' Lane
ACCESS college open daily, 13.45–16.30; also 10.15–12.45 July to September; admission charge

Mid-fifteenth to late sixteenth centuries

King's College Chapel and colleges to its south

Mid-fifteenth to late sixteenth centuries

Queens' College, Mathematical Bridge and Pump Court

Though rebuilt in 1902, the so-called 'Mathematical Bridge' is a copy of that designed by William Etheridge and built by James Essex in 1749–50 to replace an earlier bridge. Etheridge had been involved in the construction of Westminster Bridge (1744–49) in London. It may have been the timber centering for the arches there, or an earlier proposal for a timber bridge by James King, that led Etheridge to design similar bridges at Walton-on-Thames, Surrey, and at Queens' College. Timber pegs were used to join the members, and it was said that any decayed members could be replaced without endangering the structure.

James Essex was the son of a carpenter who went on to study architecture under James Burrough, and the L-shaped building around Pump Court, now known as the Essex Building, was the first of a number of his designs in Cambridge. Built to replace a court of 1564, it contains sets of Fellows' rooms on three storeys, served by a single staircase in a spacious corner stairwell. It is a carefully proportioned if rather dull building in the classical style. In total contrast with the original parts of the college, it is of local white brick with stone window surrounds and a stone balustraded parapet. The building follows the line of Silver Street, with the corner bay stepping forward as an end pavilion, and is a small part of an unrealised proposal to redevelop the entire river frontage of Queens' College in a uniform style.

ADDRESS Queens' Lane
ACCESS college open daily, 13.45–16.30; also 10.15–12.45 July to September; admission charge; visible from Silver Street Bridge

William Etheridge 1749–50, James Essex 1756–60

King's College Chapel and colleges to its south

William Etheridge 1749–50, James Essex 1756–60

Queens' College, Chapel

George Frederick Bodley had worked at Queens' College from 1858 to 1861 both in refitting the old chapel, where he removed the eighteenth-century work and rebuilt the roof in its original style, and in restoring the hall (see page 5.72). When the college decided the old chapel was no longer adequate, it again turned to Bodley, who in the meantime had completed All Saints', Jesus Lane (see page 2.16).

The chapel subdivides Walnut Tree Court, whose size was defined at that time by W M Fawcett's North Range of 1886. It adjoins the range of 1616–18 that extends Front Court to the north, whose roof was rebuilt in 1778 and 1782 after a fire. The chapel's use of red brick with stone dressings continues the language of the original college, while the battlemented parapet reflects that of the adjacent range. Like the medieval chapel for Trinity College (see page 4.84), and unlike George Gilbert Scott's 1863–69 chapel for St John's College (see page 4.72), Bodley's chapel is a simple rectangular volume without a tower or spire. Its Gothic Revival style is of the fourteenth century, about a century earlier than the college's earliest buildings. The interior is both tall and relatively narrow, and reaches a climax at the sumptuously decorated east end, providing a setting for a late fifteenth-century South German altar painting.

The range adjoining the chapel to the north was built in 1912 to designs by Henry T Hare, who also designed Westminster College (see page 1.12).

ADDRESS Queens' Lane
ACCESS college open daily, 13.45–16.30; also 10.15–12.45 July to September; admission charge

George Frederick Bodley 1889–91

George Frederick Bodley 1889–91

Queens' College, Erasmus Building

Despite its restrained design, the Erasmus Building, housing 43 undergraduates and two Fellows, was controversial when opened in 1961. Cambridge's first example of post-war modern architecture, it was designed by Basil Spence – the 1951 winner of the competition for the new Coventry Cathedral – and enjoys an especially prominent position overlooking the River Cam.

To open up views of the river from Walnut Tree Court and to provide covered areas for social occasions, Spence raised the building on massive brick piers, with concrete columns to mark the entrance. As if in response to the historic setting, the piers are joined by four-centred Tudor arches, and the L-shaped building is constructed of a mixture of red brick and stone. Cantilevered out above the piers are three storeys of rooms served by corridors, supported by load-bearing brick cross-walls. These are crowned by a roof terrace given external expression by a white-painted concrete pergola.

The language of Spence's elevations expresses the structure of the building: a band of stone masks the cantilevered concrete slab, another the roof terrace and slit windows express the ends of the cross-walls. A vertical window lighting the main staircase separates the two arms of the building when seen from the river, while other full-height slit windows divide the curiously fenestrated end façade facing the river from the main body of the block. Like many English buildings of the period influenced by the work of the Swiss architect Le Corbusier, the Erasmus Building lacks his plasticity and clarity of expression.

ADDRESS Queens' Lane
ACCESS college open daily, 13.45–16.30; also 10.15–12.45 July to September; admission charge

Basil Spence 1959–61

King's College Chapel and colleges to its south

Basil Spence 1959–61

Queens' College, Cripps Building

Both this and the architects' earlier building for St John's College (see page 4.74) bear the name of the benefactor, Humphrey Cripps. The brief was for 146 student sets plus new dining facilities and common rooms on a site adjacent to Norman Drinkwater's neo-Tudor Fisher Building of 1936.

Powell and Moya's design ignores the crescent form of the Fisher Building, preferring instead to extend the college's sequence of courts by creating a new court standing in object-like isolation. The grassed court is contained on three sides by four-storey ranges of student rooms grouped in 'houses' around top-lit staircases accessed from a cloister at ground-floor level. The architectural language shares much with Powell and Moya's earlier building for St John's College. The court, the cloister, the expressed structural frame and the roof articulation are present in both, although the detailed design varies. Here, a more delicate white precast concrete frame has replaced the monumental stone piers of the St John's building. Now it is the paired circular columns and concrete spandrel panels, with infill panels of glass and bronze, that create the strong, confident aesthetic.

The fourth side of the court contains the dining halls, common rooms and kitchen and is designed to read as a distinct pavilion. The steeply roofed, lantern-topped pavilion is cantilevered above pilotis. The distinctive glass screen to the first-floor small dining room is made up of zigzag strips of vertical glazing that diffuse the view down into the court from within. The lantern lights the elegant first-floor main dining hall.

Powell and Moya 1972–81

Powell and Moya 1972–81

Robinson College

Robinson College is the most recent college foundation in Cambridge. The challenge posed to the Glasgow architects was to suggest an appropriate physical form for a late twentieth-century college. Their solution was to produce a tough red-brick megastructure, alluding more to Scottish baronial castles than to the surrounding suburban houses. The design takes cues from the medieval college typology: its organisation is inward-looking, the exterior of the building solid and impenetrable, and the college is entered through a controlled gatehouse.

However, the architects rejected the court as the organising structure and chose instead to place the accommodation around a first-floor open-air linear spine, or 'street', which cranks to form an L-shaped building. All the college elements are present: hall, chapel, library and student accommodation, but while all are accessed from the street none has a direct dialogue with it and the result is rather private and monastic. Additionally, the relentless use of brickwork for the walls creates a severe, serious atmosphere. The external walls of the college also rise sheer and defensive on both the road and the garden side so, although the gardens are beautifully designed, the possibilities of integrating landscape and building are sadly missed.

However, moments of real delight remain. The chapel and library are beautifully lit and well-crafted spaces where references to the square motif originating from Charles Rennie Mackintosh abound.

ADDRESS Grange Road, Herschel Road
ACCESS college open Monday to Friday, 10.00–18.00; Sunday, 14.00–18.00; closed May to early June

Gillespie Kidd and Coia 1977–80

Gillespie Kidd and Coia 1977–80

St Catherine's College, Principal Court

In 1674 a decision was taken to rebuild St Catherine's College. By 1675 the west end of the north range had been rebuilt, although the present Gothic-style windows and the bay window to the hall are of 1868. The west end of the south range was completed by 1678, and the shell of the west range along Queens' Lane by 1679. The central three-storey baroque frontispiece marks the college's original entrance from Queens' Lane. The new buildings are in dark red brick, with stone windows and quoins, and have three storeys with attics. These have alternating triangular and segmental pediments. The windows have cross-shaped mullions and transoms, a type that the master mason Robert Grumbold also used at Clare College shortly afterwards (see page 4.14).

The chapel, completing the north range, was built next in 1694–1704. Although William Talman was consulted, Grumbold was again the designer. The four large pedimented windows of the south elevation are reminiscent of his Clare College hall, but the classical east elevation is more ambitious. The baroque oak fittings by Taylor of London are original and particularly fine, with the exception of the Victorian organ.

In 1756–72 James Essex completed the south range in a matching style. Shortly afterwards the hostelries between the court and Trumpington Street were cleared away, making a new entrance to the college, and it was decided not to build the projected east range: the gate and railings date from 1779. This decision was respected when in 1930 and 1949 flanking pavilions in eighteenth-century baroque were added to the north and south of the college on Trumpington Street.

ADDRESS Trumpington Street
ACCESS apply at porter's lodge; closed May and June

Robert Grumbold 1674–87, 1694–1704, James Essex 1756–72

King's College Chapel and colleges to its south

Robert Grumbold 1674–87, 1694–1704, James Essex 1756–72

Selwyn College

Selwyn College was founded in 1882 in memory of Augustus Selwyn, Bishop of New Zealand and later of Lichfield, with the aim of preserving Anglican culture. Arthur Blomfield, an active church architect at the height of his career, designed a spacious court in Tudor-Gothic, built of red brick with stone dressings under a steeply pitched slate roof enlivened with gables, half dormers and tall chimney stacks. Compared with nearby Newnham College (see page 5.46) started eight years earlier, the style is austere and traditional.

The west range fronting Grange Road, with its prominent asymmetrical gate tower, was built first in 1882, followed by the Master's Lodge in the south-east corner of the court in 1883. In 1884 the west end of the north range was built, and the range was completed in 1889. The chapel, axially opposite the gatehouse, followed in 1893–95. The west front, although with horizontal bands of stone and brick, is reminiscent of the west front of King's College Chapel (see page 5.36). Internally, the use of the same materials under an open timber roof gives the chapel a distinctly spartan feeling, despite the fine timber stalls and panelling.

Sidgwick Avenue to the south of the court was opened up in 1891, but the court was only closed on that side in 1909 by the construction of the hall, designed by Messrs Grayson and Ould in the Jacobean style. In 1959 James Stirling and James Gowan produced designs for a new residential building consisting of a four-storey faceted glass wall snaking around the perimeter of the college's gardens, but this proposal remained unrealised.

ADDRESS Grange Road, near Sidgwick Avenue
ACCESS apply at porter's lodge

Arthur Blomfield 1882–95

King's College Chapel and colleges to its south

Arthur Blomfield 1882–95

The District

Ely Cathedral

Ely Cathedral, placed along the top of the low hill that dominates the surrounding flat fen land, is an unforgettable sight.

Of the Norman monastic cathedral the transepts are the earliest surviving parts. The early twelfth-century nave of 12 bays is tall, narrow and long, with massive columns and round-arched openings characteristic of the Norman period. The west front was built a little after the nave. Unusually it consists of a central tower with a south transept terminated by two ten-sided turrets, all heavily arcaded. Originally there was a matching north transept, and the tower had a spire, which was replaced in the late fourteenth century with the present top stage. The two-storey Galilee porch was added in the early thirteenth century.

The Norman chancel was rebuilt in 1234–52 in the early Gothic style to house more magnificently the shrine of St Etheldreda. The arches are pointed and heavily moulded, the columns have attached piers, the carving is stiff-leafed and there is a many-ribbed stone vault. The collapse in 1322 of the Norman crossing tower resulted in Ely's most remarkable and spatially inventive feature. In 1322–37 Alan of Walsingham greatly enlarged the crossing to form an octagon, above which a massive timber lantern, allowing light to flood in, appears to float on soaring timber ribs. The first three bays of the chancel, demolished by the collapse, were rebuilt in 1328–35 in the same more delicate Gothic style.

An almost separate Lady Chapel was built to the north of the choir in c.1335–53. Beneath an intricate lierne vault large windows fill the rectangular space with light, showing off the elaborate late-Gothic carving and double ogee arches.

ADDRESS Ely, 26 kilometres north of Cambridge by the A30
ACCESS daily, summer 7.00–19.00; winter 7.00–17.00

Early twelfth–fourteenth centuries

Early twelfth–fourteenth centuries

Wimpole Hall

Wimpole Hall, set in a landscaped park, is not only the largest house in Cambridgeshire, but also the most important as regards the sheer number of celebrated architects and landscape gardeners who worked there. It consists of a three-storey entrance block seven bays wide with lower flanking wings, and further projecting wings on the garden side. It is in red brick with stone dressings, in a plain classical style.

The side wings were designed by James Gibbs and built in 1713–30. The chapel in the east wing was decorated in 1724 with *trompe l'oeil* paintings by James Thornhill. Gibbs also designed the main staircase and the west garden wing with its double-cube library, and refaced the garden front of the central block. In 1742–45 Henry Flitcroft refaced the entrance front of the earlier central block to match the flanking wings, although the central pediment and parapets date only from 1842. Flitcroft also remodelled much of the interior, adding the bay window to the centre of the garden side. The east garden wing and the matching bay windows were added later in the century.

The most memorable interiors at Wimpole are those remodelled in 1791–93 to designs by the young John Soane. His Book Room in Gibbs's west wing presents a progression of segmental arches between projecting bookcases. Soane's double-height Yellow Drawing Room is a double square on plan with two semicircular apses, lit by a circular lantern supported by a delicately fluted dome. Soane inserted a new staircase, remodelled the top of Gibbs's staircase and added a charming Bath House.

ADDRESS Wimpole Hall, Arrington, 15 kilometres south-west of Cambridge by the A603
ACCESS open Easter to 1 November, Tuesday to Thursday, Saturday, Sunday and Bank Holidays, 13.00–17.00; admission charge

James Gibbs 1713–30, Henry Flitcroft 1742–45, John Soane 1791–93

James Gibbs 1713–30, Henry Flitcroft 1742–45, John Soane 1791–

Impington Village College

Impington was one of a number of progressive educational establishments known as village colleges built in Cambridgeshire in the inter-war period under the direction of its chief educational officer Henry Morris. They were conceived to serve a number of surrounding villages and to provide a greatly extended system of education for all ages, now called community education. Impington was the first to be built and Morris was determined to commission a progressive architect for the design, hence the choice of Maxwell Fry and Walter Gropius, the latter being one-time head of the Bauhaus in Weimar and an exile from Hitler's Germany.

Impington is architecturally the most interesting of the 17 village colleges. The composition is picturesque: single-storey classroom wings extending into the parkland setting to produce open courts. The wings are linked by a wide corridor or 'promenade'. A dramatic two-storey fan-shaped hall with a daring reinforced concrete cantilevered canopy marks the main entrance. The progressive architectural ideas include the cross-ventilated classrooms with adjacent outdoor teaching areas, external walkways and the use of contemporary products such as metal casement windows and under-floor heating. Otherwise the construction is of rather straightforward load-bearing brickwork walls with a flat steel roof structure.

Nikolaus Pevsner in *Buildings of England* described the college as 'one of the best buildings of its date in England, if not the best', but this could be interpreted as a comment on the paucity of inter-war modern architecture in England compared with the contemporary European scene.

ADDRESS Impington Hall Estate, Impington, 5 kilometres north of Cambridge by the B1049
ACCESS none; visible from the street

Walter Gropius and Maxwell Fry 1938

Walter Gropius and Maxwell Fry 1938

American Military Cemetery

The American Military Cemetery was laid out under the auspices of the American Battle Monuments Commission, on a 12.3-hectare site given by the university, to designs of an appropriately austere minimal classicism by the Boston firm Percy, Shaw, Hepburn, Kehoe & Dean.

The beautifully landscaped site revolves around a flagpole that signals the entrance, whence the headstones fan out in radiating arcs across mown lawns towards the rolling countryside. Along the highest part of the site, parallel with the road, is an east–west axial mall which, starting with the flagpole, leads past a series of rectangular reflecting pools and is terminated by the tall gable end of the chapel. A continuous wall of memory, sheltered by a belt of woodland, runs along its south side, while to the north are views under trees over the cemetery. The main body of the chapel is a museum room whose solid south wall is carved with a campaign map, and whose north wall consists of five pylons with glazing, again opening up views over the cemetery and the countryside beyond. The altar beyond sits in an apse decorated with mosaic.

The buildings and walls are all of white Portland stone, square-cut and entirely without ornament which, together with the directness of the layout, gives the site a restrained dignity.

ADDRESS St Neots Road, Madingley, 5 kilometres west of Cambridge on the A14
ACCESS daily, summer 8.00–18.00, winter 8.00–17.00

Perry Stuart and Hepburn, Kehoe and Dean 1952–54

Perry Stuart and Hepburn, Kehoe and Dean 1952–54

Patcentre

The architects' well-established 'high-tech' approach, made famous by their Centre Georges Pompidou in Paris (1971–77), attracted this commission from PA International Management Consultants who wanted a flagship headquarters to express their corporate image of integrated working practices and creative innovation. The brief consisted of a mix of research laboratories, workshops and administration areas.

From the sinuous approach footpath from the car park the building reads as a simple low box sitting calmly within undulating fields. Closer inspection reveals that the box is raised above a dark undercroft that rather unceremoniously houses the service areas and workshop. The entrance lies near the centre of the north elevation and leads into a double-height reception atrium from which a tubular steel staircase leads up to the main floor. Here the laboratories and other compartmented accommodation occupy the core area, while the perimeter houses support areas in an appropriately light and open atmosphere. The main floor of the building and its supporting columns are of in-situ concrete, and cruciform precast concrete columns support a light two-way steel roof structure. Internal partitions are lightweight and demountable. The external cladding consists of a primary framework of steel that accepts either glazed or vitreous enamelled sandwich panels. Services are suspended under the floor slab and they feed through a regular grid of knockout plugs. This architecture of assembly, although not always an appropriate solution, here seems to fulfil admirably the client's wish for flexibility, expansion and modernity.

ADDRESS Back Lane, Melbourn, 16 kilometres south-west of Cambridge by the A10
ACCESS none; visible from the approach road

Renzo Piano and Richard Rogers 1975–83 (three phases)

Renzo Piano and Richard Rogers 1975–83 (three phases)

American Air Museum

Some idea of the sheer size of Norman Foster's shell-like museum hangar at Duxford is gained from the fact that, in addition to many other aeroplanes, it easily houses a B-52 Stratofortress bomber with its 61-metre wingspan. Like a giant half-open eye, ever watchful in best Cold War tradition, the hangar stares out over the rolling landscape.

The approach, past several other exhibition hangars aligned alongside the First World War airfield, leads to a curving grassy mound through which a tunnel enters the centre of the building from the rear. From this, elevated ramps glide down to floor level each side of the half-elliptical plan, allowing ever-changing views of the exhibits. Above the ramps, a continuous glazing strip divides the perimeter of the roof shell from the wall of the surrounding earthworks, behind which are housed ancillary spaces at ground level.

Two thicknesses of precast concrete panels form the shell roof, separated by beams cast into the lower panels. The concrete provides not only thermal mass, contributing to humidity control in the unheated volume, but also adequate strength for aeroplanes to be suspended seemingly in mid-flight. The outward forces of the shell are contained by an in-situ concrete ring beam that follows the top of the earth mound at the rear of the building. At the front, the shell forms a shallow arch over a huge expanse of glazed wall that floods the building with natural light, and is designed to be removable to allow exhibits to be changed. This is an elegantly engineered way of enclosing a vast, low-maintenance volume.

ADDRESS Imperial War Museum, Duxford, 13 kilometres south of Cambridge by the M11, junction 10
ACCESS daily, summer 10.00–18.00, winter 10.00–16.00

Foster & Partners 1997–98

Foster & Partners 1997–98

Index

Index

Cambridge: an architectural guide

Index